How to Write and Share Humor:

Techniques to Tickle Funny Bones

and Win Fans

How to Write and Share Humor:

Techniques to Tickle Funny Bones

and Win Fans

Donna Cavanagh

Cover design by Dwayne Booth. Book design by HumorOutcasts Press.

Author photo by Pam Baumann Photography

Published 2016 by HumorOutcasts Press
Printed in the United States of America

ISBN: 0-692-72282-3
EAN-13: 978-069272282-4

DEDICATION:

To Carol Sabik-Jaffe and the wonderful people at the Philadelphia Writers' Conference and its humor workshop class of 2014. Thanks for asking me to put the workshop into book form. Never before have I taught such an inspiring group!

To my wonderful writers at HumorOutcasts.com How lucky I am to have you all! You make being an HO a lot of fun.

ACKNOWLEDGEMENTS:

Putting together a book is never easy so I want to thank my technical wizards, Ed Cavanagh, my dogs Frankie and Lulu (yes, they keep my office going) and any other consultants who have come to my rescue with their excellent formatting skills.

Big shout outs to Dwayne Booth, who again delivered an amazing cover design and Pam Baumann of Pam Baumann Photography, who quieted my fear of cameras and gave me a great photo!

Thank you to Bill Spencer for reading, critiquing and supporting this effort. Karma will return to you tenfold.

Thanks to Dr. Nancy Berk for also lending her eyes to make sure I didn't bore people too much

and finally,

a big hug to the humorists who responded to my request to submit an essay. So grateful to you all.

Contents

Cartoon by Phillip Dillman, author of *Scripture Scribbles: Cartoons from the Choir Loft,* and *More Scripture Scribbles: Cartoons from the Choir Loft.*

Foreword
By Jamie Reidy

We find humor in funny places. Sometimes, even in child neglect.

In March of 2005, I published "Hard Sell: The Evolution of a Viagra Salesman," a lighthearted memoir of my time working for Pfizer and selling little blue pills.

Reviewers from more than fifty outlets including *The New York Times, Fortune* and CNBC all read the book.

My mother did not.

She stopped less than ten-percent in, upset that I'd given "away too many family secrets." (btw, I didn't think it was some big revelation that my old man enjoys several Irish Coffees after Christmas dinner.)

The fact that Mom had yet to read it never occurred to me, since I had been operating under the clearly delusional assumption that she'd read the 225 inkjet-printed pages I'd mailed my parents two years prior, as soon as I'd completed my draft. Apparently, the many other books my siblings had already published left her uninspired to peruse mine. Oh, wait; neither my brother nor my sister had ever published anything. Hmmmm. My folks simply did not feel compelled to read my manuscript, letting the binder collect dust in the basement not far from the clothes hanger/exercise bike.

I only learned about my mother's failure to read her firstborn's first book because her middle child happened to be visiting home when she'd cracked the hard cover's spine. The instant I heard my brother's voice on the phone, I knew something funny had occurred. I also sensed I was the butt of the joke. Patrick happily relayed to me that he had witnessed Mom both begin and cease reading "Hard Sell." Unable to contain his glee, he informed me that "the ratio of cigarette drags and sips of pinot grigio to pages read was unsustainable." Finally, she closed the book at page 17. It remained closed for five years, during which time she read a few hundred sci-fi and trashy romance novels.

In the interim, executives in Hollywood read the book, resulting in a bidding war between two studios. I sold the film rights to 20th Century Fox. (Pro tip: when describing somebody else's deal, you say, "movie rights to Fox." But when it's your deal, you emphasize "film" and specify every word in the studio's name.) The screenwriter, Charles Randolph, crafted a story *very* loosely based on my memoir. (Note: there was no need to mention Charles here, but since he just won an Oscar for co-writing "The Big Short," I shamelessly name-dropped. Amazing what that guy can do with quality source material, huh?)

Just before the movie *Love and Other Drugs* starring Jake Gyllenhaal and Anne Hathaway premiered, my mother decided to read my book "to see what the big deal is." Unfortunately, she did not see the big deal. At my premiere, Mom did, however, see on the big screen naked people having a lot of sex. At the after party, she ditched the pinot grigio for Johnny Walker Red.

I just realized Donna, who welcomed me into the Humoroutcasts.com family three years ago, has asked me to pen a humor book foreword, not an application for a new therapist. My apologies. Please know I'll be sure to mention this gaffe in my first session.

Here's my advice for writing humor: Write what makes you laugh.

Your mother probably won't read it anyway.

Jamie Reidy graduated from the University of Notre Dame and served with distinction as a U.S. Army officer... before becoming an author and an embarrassment to his parents. His first book, Hard Sell: The Evolution of A Viagra Salesman, served as the basis for the movie Love and Other Drugs, starring Jake Gyllenhaal. Nobody wanted to turn either of Jamie's next two books into movies.

Introduction

I didn't start out to be a humor writer. I didn't start out to be a writer at all. I always liked to write, and my teachers told me I possessed the talent, but never in my wildest dreams did I think that writing would be my chosen profession. However, somehow my life took this sharp turn down a steep hill and bulldozed its way into journalism, business writing and dare I say it—humor.

A few years into my journalism career, I wrote a funny piece for our paper's holiday party making harmless fun of the editor-in-chief. When the editor, who resembled a bald version of the cigar-chomping Perry White of the Daily Planet, read the piece, he summoned me into his office. I was scared. I worked night-side or the 6 PM to 2 AM shift, so for the big guy to summon me back to the paper for 8:30 AM, it could only mean I was toast. I braced for the axe to fall; however, I was relieved to find out that he found the entire column laugh-out-loud funny, which stunned me because I didn't think the man knew how to laugh out loud. Much to my surprise, he asked for more humor for the paper.

Not long after this meeting, I resigned my post as a general reporter. With a toddler at home, my husband in graduate school and the night shift turning me into a zombie, I needed a change in my life—quickly. I adapted well to my new non-deadline life, but after about a week of appreciating the fact that it was normal for people to walk around during the day and sleep during the dark hours, I got itchy to write again. I took my editor's words to heart and submitted humor pieces to every local paper I could find. Within a month, another daily paper offered me my own column. I was floored at the opportunity and for five years, my column *The Lighter Side* ran bi-weekly. I wrote about my family, current events, politics…anything that I thought might create a chuckle. My column received a lot of attention and some hate mail, but that's how it goes with humor. When a newspaper chain bought all the local papers in the area, they essentially syndicated my column. That corporate merger catapulted me to a national audience where I became a regular humorist for *First* Magazine, which helped me find further opportunities with regional and national media.

But as they say, all good things come to an end. The internet came, newspapers downsized and so my column was no more. A switch in editorial staff at the magazine prompted them to go to the tear-jerker stories of cancer, divorce, etc. It broke my heart to think that humor was considered passé.

Although writing humor was now on the back burner, I never stopped freelancing. I made a good living doing business articles, public relations interviews and brochures, but I missed making people laugh. While surfing the net, I found several sites that would allow me to share my humor. I joined Associated Content (which is now Yahoo which is now nothing like it was years ago) and other sites. For two years, I wrote humor, made great friends and published several humor books, one of which (*Life on the Off Ramp*) became a USA Books finalist. I enjoyed the lift that humor writing gave me. (Feel free to put this book aside for a few seconds and check out my other books on Amazon.com. Yes, I'm not too proud to ask. If it means a book sale, I'm good.) But a conservative element invaded those sites, and humor writers noticed their work being flagged or removed. In frustration, I decided that I wanted to create a site where humor writers could be free, or almost free, from censorship.

Since our defecting humor clan considered ourselves to be OUTCASTS, I named the site HumorOutcasts.com failing to take into account two things: 1) the site would take off and only a few people would get the history behind the name OUTCASTS and 2) HumorOutcasts would be shortened to HO, and we would forever be known as the HOs. At Christmas, it's not bad because we can be HO, HO, HO, but for most of the year we get inquiries on what kind of "special" services we provide.

Let's fast forward. Within two years, HO blossomed from a site with five writers to a site with more than 100 writers who enjoyed a place where they could spread their creative wings. The site accepted writers who ranged from "newbies" to well-established and award-winning TV comedy writers, producers, authors, standup comics, filmmakers and columnists. Our reads grew from 300 a day to 3,000 a day to sometimes as high as 20,000. It proved to be a great deal of fun and a lot of work for both me and my editor Betsy.

Ah…Betsy. Did I mention her yet? Okay, this is the skinny on Betsy. I made her up. I wanted HO to be a submission site, which meant some people were going to get rejected. We couldn't accept every writer, or else HO would turn into the mess that many of the bigger sites had become. Plus, my goal was to build audiences for my writers and how could I do that if I let everyone on the site? I needed someone who could reject writers, and I did not have the proverbial "balls" to carry out that task. But Betsy did. It wasn't hard creating the persona. Elizabeth is my middle name and Dickinson is for Emily Dickinson, my favorite poet. As it turned out, Betsy was a natural on social media, and she thrived. She had her own Facebook page, and she ran HumorOutcasts with an iron but gentle hand. She led quite the life. She was a USC graduate who liked the great outdoors. A gay friend who knew about Betsy asked me to make her a lesbian, so poof! she was a lesbian. Needless to say, everything was okay until Betsy started to get asked to do interviews, was nominated for a media award and received lots of requests for alumni contributions from her alma mater.

Who knew I could be jealous over my alter ego's success! And on top of all the hoopla, I was mixing up my identities. I was answering Betsy's emails in my Donna voice and vice versa. I decided it was time for Betsy to go. She was becoming more trouble than she was worth, so it became plain to see that I had to kill her off. I had envisioned this great dramatic ending where she would be lost spelunking in some massive cave in Utah while honeymooning with her lesbian lover. I thought that since she lived life with such gusto, she should die the same way. In the end, Betsy decided she wanted to go out quietly. Yes, she told me that…don't judge me.

While Betsy no longer exists, her social media accounts do, and very few people have noticed that she's officially gone. She still gets email, and I still answer it. But if it is hate mail from an offended reader—a daily occurrence when one runs a humor site—I just tell the "offended" that we are sorry they don't like HO, but we don't care since we are in mourning as Betsy died suddenly. That bit of sad news usually throws the haters off balance and makes them feel like crap which brightens my day. I think had I gone through with Betsy's faux funeral, her demise would have had a more lasting effect, but Betsy didn't take advantage of the discounted final expenses insurance offered by her supposed alma mater, and I'm pretty sure the IRS would have frowned upon my taking the funeral as a business expense, so we settled on a private service, which in truth was no service at all.

Rewind just a bit: Two years after HO hit the internet scene, some of my writers asked if I could help them publish their books. What they found out was the publishing world had changed and humor, while always a pariah for publishers, had reached a new level of "pariahdom." In fact, rumor has it that publishers and literary agents hung garlic outside their doors to stave off the unwanted advances of humor writers seeking representation. Yes, we were the vampires and undead of the literary world and not the six-pack, sexy vampires of the movies today. No, we were the icky, creepy ones that gave us nightmares as children. And this is how our partner publishing house HumorOutcasts Press was born. We didn't hang out garlic. We welcomed humorists into our fold, and as our catalog grew, so did requests for publishing services from non-humor authors. Not wanting to shut out any talented writer, we expanded our services to include Shorehouse Books for non-humor genres (HOPress-ShorehouseBooks.com). Again, I was in the right place at the right time because three years later, we have more than 40 titles available, authors contacting us daily for help and a business imprint, Corner Office Books, in production.

What does all this have to do with me teaching you about writing humor? Well, as it turns out, twenty-plus years of my stories, experiences and publishing credentials made me in demand for teaching gigs at writing conferences such as the Philadelphia Writers' Conference and the Erma Bombeck Writers' Workshop. It was in Philadelphia where my class—those wonderfully receptive and inspiring people who stayed with me for three days—asked me to transform the workshop into this book. So, almost two years later, here it is.

This book is not meant to be a textbook. It is a guide for budding and established writers who want to know more about writing humor essays or bringing humor into speeches or non-humor articles. My original title for this book was *What I Have Learned in My More Than Twenty Years of Humor Writing*, but that title didn't pass the beta test. But it did express the theme of the book quite well. I have separated the book into three sections:

Part I focuses on my workshop topics, which encompass mostly the construction of humor essays as well as articles with an infusion of humor. I will cover everything from developing an idea to building an essay using "humor helpers." As I said above, if you are a non-humorist looking to bring a bit of laughter into an article or speech, the techniques in this book will help you too. This book does not go into the world of comedy novels or large works of fiction. I will leave that task for another time. I wanted this book to be an easy-to-follow, first stepping stone on the path to humor.

Part II of this book shares my experiences about building a humor audience. In this section, I will discuss avenues for your writing such as blogging, the types of blogs and how to build audiences through social media. I will go through some social media tips for the various platforms that are out there such as Facebook, Twitter, Pinterest, StumbleUpon and LinkedIn.

Part III of this book will talk about the new and exciting publishing world for those who are ready to take that next step. Every day, I hear from writers who lament the fact they can't get a publisher. There are options, and this book is going to talk about them.

I hope this book gives you the confidence and tools to take on the humor genre. I hope you realize what I realized years ago—that humor is not the bane of the publishing world, but the jewel of the publishing world. Humor is an essential part of life. It gives us the strength to survive the worst crises. It allows us to keep going day after day even if we binge watch FOX News and are scared out of our wits. Humor is our lifeline. In short, which I might be in stature but never in word count, humor is serious business, and we should never underestimate its power or value.

My journey through humor has made me not only a writer but a mentor as well. There is a connotation to the word "mentor," and it's a commitment I don't take lightly. I tell my writers and those aspiring writers to contact me. I'm okay with that. If you need some advice, the sound of a human voice (writing is such a solitary activity), you can email me, and we can set up a time to chat. Don't be afraid to reach out. If you get a response from Betsy, be very afraid and run for the hills, but on a positive note, she will pass on the message.

As a bonus for this book, I added *Humor Inspiration* pages. These are contributions from some of the writers of HumorOutcasts.com, my HOPress-Shorehouse Books authors and other humorists I admire as well. No two humorists are the same in how they approach their craft. It's fun to learn about different writers and their process and what inspires them to do the "humor thing."

So in closing, here's to the wonder of humor. May you see it in your everyday life, and may you want to share it with the world.

Donna
www.HumorOutcasts.com
Donna@humoroutcasts.com

PART I: CAN I WRITE FUNNY?

Some writers do not know they are funny. Some writers can't put their funny into words, and some want to use humor to loosen up their audience. How hard is it to write funny?

CHAPTER I: Let's Talk Humor

A few years ago, while surfing the net, I came across this great quote from author and literary analyst Michael Cart. I found Mr. Cart on LinkedIn and asked him to follow me, but I got no response. However, in his defense, and as anyone on LinkedIn knows, if a person you don't know asks you to be a connection, that person is probably a stalker. Yep, LinkedIn is the most paranoid social media platform available, and it makes people crazy with suspicion, but I still like it.

Anyway, back to the quote from Michael Cart, which I assume is correct because I did read it on the internet and everything you read on the internet is true so...

"Humor is the Rodney Dangerfield of Literary genres. It gets no respect."

That quote blew me away. It is so profound that it deserved to be centered, italicized and put in quotation marks. And it is one hundred percent true. We all know we like to laugh. We watch comedians, sitcoms and funny movies. Our Facebook feeds are saturated with funny pictures, headlines and witty sayings. While I have no scientific data to back this next statement up, I would guess that humor is the fourth most popular type of post on Facebook. Posts about puppies, kittens and, of course, the consumption of wine seem to grab the top three spots.

Despite its amazing popularity, humor still is the black sheep of the literary world. It's a mystery as to why this is. My guess is that those in the "real writing and reading world" put down humor because they struggle writing humor, and that fact ticks them off.

HUMOR IS ONE OF THE MOST DIFFICULT GENRES TO WRITE

I don't mean to burst your bubble so soon out of the starting gate, but a lot of people do NOT write humor well. And I'm not just talking about the ability to write jokes or humorous essays. I'm talking about possessing the ability to infuse humor into their work even a tiny bit. It's a difficult task and not for the weak hearted. Humor, if not done well and even if done well, can be misconstrued, judged or viewed as offensive. So you have to be careful with your words and project how they will affect your life and those in your life.

Who should not write humor?
- Anyone who hates to laugh
- Anyone who finds no humor in everyday life
- Anyone who needs to be liked all the time
- Anyone who is afraid to be offensive
- Anyone who must declare out loud to the world as often as possible how hysterically funny he or she is (if you have to keep telling people you are hysterical, there's a better than ninety percent chance you are not hysterical).

What are some of the major challenges to writing humor?
- It is hard to translate the cadence of spoken word to written word.
- It is hard to create descriptions that paint your story in a humorous way.
- It is hard to create dialogue that represents the tone of the story you want to tell.
- It is hard to let go of inhibitions that have plagued you since you left the womb.

- Don't fret. In this book, we will cover many of these challenges for you. So take a deep breath and read on.

CHAPTER II: To Niche or Not Niche

I guess if we want to truly understand the humor genre, we should start at the beginning and ask

"What is humor?" I could give you the dry dictionary definition, but that's boring. Instead, I'm going to give you my definition. Humor makes us smile, chuckle or laugh so hard coffee shoots out our noses when we read and drink at the same time. Humor tickles our funny bones and transforms a bad mood into a good mood. Humor is powerful stuff. In case anyone is wondering, comedy is a category under humor and is defined as a humorous art form, which can be written or oral and results in physical laughter. There are also many sub-genres of humor. Some of the more popular include:

- Observational Humor - Finding comedy in everyday life from your neighbor's habit of walking around outside in his underwear to funny road signs
- Situational Humor - From trips to the emergency room to getting pulled over for a ticket to finding snakes in your bed—sure they sound terrible, but if they are not happening to you, they can be pretty funny.
- Satire - Making fun of culture, society, politics, religion, etc.
- Bathroom Humor - Fart and poop jokes never to go out of style.
- Relationship and Family Humor - Spouse and kids and all that goes with these topics, plus dating and divorce

- Stage of Life Humor - This can sometimes overlap with relationship humor as it encompasses topics such as empty nest, middle-age crisis, mommy bloggers, widowhood and menopause.
- Caustic or Snarky Humor (takes no hostages) - No one is protected from witty barbs.
- Melting Pot Humor - In this category I include everything from silly or funny photos with captions to fictional essays.

Do I have to find a niche?

Let's assume you have the gift for humor but you don't know what to do with this gift. The number one question budding humorists ask is "What should I write about?" I might be a rebel here, but this is my take on this sensitive topic. From day one in classrooms, kids and adults are taught "WRITE WHAT YOU KNOW." I'm not against this advice for beginners, but I am against that advice if two years down the road, you are still writing only what you know. Talk about boring. Writing is fluid; writing is a journey. Make sure you book the trip and take that journey to the unknown or else you might find yourself stuck in a pile of mediocrity with no hope of escape. That sounds so dramatic, right? Okay, you might not die in a pile of mediocrity, but you will be trapped until you get the guts to try some fresh material. Take some chances!

I hear what you are saying: "I need a niche; I need a niche." And, yes, to an extent that is true. You are not going to write about being a single dad if you are a polygamist with twenty-two kids. You are not going to write medical humor if you vomit when you get a paper cut. However, recognize the limitation to your niche. You cannot still be a "mommy blogger" when your kids have received their own AARP cards. You cannot be known as the menopause maven when your hot flashes and dry vagina turned cold a decade ago. In other words, it's the theory of Natural Selection: adapt or become extinct. Be creative, move on, push that envelope and find your funny elsewhere. It's okay to leave a niche behind so you can grow as a writer.

One other point while we are talking about what to write. Humor does not mean your entire life has to be an open book. Sure, write about experiences, but be careful. Not everyone in your life will delight in the fact that they are put on public display. Learn the difference between writing about experiences in a humorous way and humiliating your friends, family and possibly yourself.

Writing Exercise:
　　Write down what makes you laugh. Why do you find these topics so funny? Can you come up with five subjects that tickle your funny bone? Turn that idea into five sentences.

_____

_____

_____

_____

_____

_____

CHAPTER III: Rules of the Humor Road

Are there any rules for humor?
Yes. You might not like them, but here they are:

Rule #1: Trust your gut

Writers long for approval, but alas, writers are in a profession where that approval is not so easy to come by—especially when it comes to humor. Why? Humor is subjective. What you find funny, your mother or best friend might hate. There is no scientific way to figure out who will laugh at what, so you are on your own as a writer. YOU HAVE TO RELY ON YOU AND YOU ALONE. You cannot be funny if you are trying to appease each individual's sense of humor. Face the fact that not everyone is going to like you or what you write. You will be at your best when you trust your own gut and stop looking for approval. When you write for your sense of humor, you stand the best chance of keeping your work fresh and also attracting new people to your work.

I know writers who send out their work to at least 10 people before they submit it anywhere, and they are always crushed when at least five of those people want to edit it, critique it or just plain hate it. To these writers I say, "You got what you deserve. You broke the cardinal rule of writing. You wrote for someone else and not yourself. You lost your voice."

When I write a humor piece, I read it aloud and if it makes me laugh, I go with it. I am no different from other writers. I suffer the same insecurities and need for approval, but after almost thirty years in this business, I have learned to push those feelings aside and trust myself. Am I always successful? NOPE. I wrote some pieces that sank faster than the Titanic. They didn't work. I don't know why they didn't work. Maybe the people reading the paper or magazine did not subscribe to my politics, religious views or attitudes of life— or perhaps they don't embrace the same sense of humor. This happens. Get over it and move on and NEVER let the "clunkers" sabotage your gut instinct.

Rule #2: Read humor; read drama; read

I read mysteries and thrillers. Yes, I write humor, but I am addicted to mystery novels. Why? Because they give me the chance to step back and see life through another genre. Mysteries keep me thinking, which keeps me writing, which keeps me creating more humor pieces. Mysteries might have nothing to do with humor but they spur my creative soul.

I also read other humorists. I don't read a lot of them because I find that in today's world of easy posting on the internet, there is a lot of repetition, and I get bored. But I love to read non-famous or "newbie" writers, and the reason for this is that these non-established writers often possess more enthusiasm than a humorist who has written the best seller or the hit sitcom or screenplay. There is nothing like the enthusiasm of someone starting out. It's engaging, contagious and courageous.

Rule #3: Open your eyes to see the funny in almost every life moment or event

Not all events in life offer oodles of funny, but in almost any experience, we can find a hint of humor. In other words, the event might not be funny, but the cast of characters and the situations that develop around an event might present humor. For example: Your elderly uncle dies. All your extended family goes to the service. These are people you only see at weddings and funerals so what happens? You catch up with them. You laugh; you reminisce; you poke fun at the Elvis impersonator who came to the wake; you talk about your vacation and the shark encounter you had scuba diving; you laugh when someone trips into the coffin and makes the body jump. Hey, stuff happens. The event itself is not funny, but what goes on around the event can have its humorous moments. I am not saying to be disrespectful. I am saying that sadness brings humor to the surface. We need humor even in the toughest situations.

This brings up another point that many budding humorists ask: Can I write about anything? Is there any topic that is off limits?

I would say, personal experiences are yours to share and it's your decision to share them with humor or no humor. Usually, when a writer shares a sad event in his or her life and introduces humor into the mix as a way to deal with that sad event, readers get it. They understand that humor in many situations possesses therapeutic qualities.

Personally, I don't write about or poke fun at catastrophic occurrences. I am not saying they are always off limits, because good satirists or humorists can show with their words why these events should never repeat. Another important aspect of humor is that it dispels fear, and once fear becomes neutralized and people laugh, the world has more hope. So humor in these situations can be healing. There is a definite fine line when pairing catastrophe and humor. There are many talented humorists and satirists who know how to walk that line with skill. Since I am one of those people who can't text and walk at the same time, I choose to leave some topics to those more talented than I am.

So, if you are not comfortable on that tight rope, don't jump on it. Some topics will always be fodder for the humor mill and these include politics, politicians, corporations, high-profile celebrities, sex scandals, etc. Sorry to say, but once people put themselves into the limelight, they have to expect some degree of comic criticism.

Is anyone a target for humor?

I know humorists who create family members for their work because their real families would die of humiliation if they came to life in comic essays or columns. So know your targets before you expose them to the world. Maybe Aunt Gladys does not want your readers to know she has webbed feet, or maybe Cousin Willy is not proud of the fact he did a nickel in the joint for loan sharking. (Can you tell I watch ID TV?)

Rule #4: Carry a notebook

Yes, have one with you all the time. Ideas will come to you when you least expect it and if you don't write them down, you will forget. You will say, "Ok, I'll remember that." But you won't. And don't rely on your smartphone or tablet to keep these ideas. I don't know the science behind it, but there is something about pen to paper that truly starts the inspiration flowing. Go to the dollar store and buy a small notepad that can fit in your pocket or purse and a pen—they still make both. Wait until you see what your observations unlock in your mind! You will be astounded—some of you might be frightened—and if you are one of the frightened, there are quite a few self-help books that can address these thoughts too.

Rule #5: Meditate

Uh oh! I said that word and half the readers said, "Another artsy fartsy writer" while tossing this book away. But come back. This is painless; I promise. You don't have to contort your body into weird positions or light incense or even develop a mantra word. You just have to learn to relax and let your mind go. Let's learn a few things about meditation from an expert and then you can decide to follow this rule or not.

"Meditation can be a life changing practice. It is beneficial for so many aspects of life. I am particularly fond of mindfulness meditation as it is about non-judgmental awareness of the present moment. Meditation lowers blood pressure, reduces anxiety and depression, decreases tension related pain, increases serotonin- production which improves mood and behavior and improves the immune system.

With regular meditation practice (it can be just 10 minutes a day) meditation changes your brain. It brings the brainwave patterns into a relaxed state that promotes a feeling of greater clarity, calmness, joy and creativity.

In order to get in touch with your inner comedian, meditation is a direct highway to that part of your brain. We are so often in our heads (dwelling in the past or worrying about the future) and that is of no help to us ever, especially when we are writing. Those fears and worries create mental blocks to our inner well of creative juice. When we release that by coming back in to the present moment (which meditation helps us do) we are able to access that part of ourselves more freely."

Melissa Schnapp is founder and president of LifeStep Coaching, LLC.

See, I knew this would make you want to find a quiet place to rest and cleanse your brain

Rule #6: Let go of the conventional grammar rules
Part of the problem to humor gaining little respect from the academic community is that humorists take liberties with grammar. And we have to do that. Humor is one of the few genres where you can throw some of the grammar rules out the window. Humorists need the freedom to play with words and dialogue to bring home the funny. In a perfect world, perfect grammar would make us giggle, but it does not. So, for those who need official dispensation to go AWOL from grammar rules for the sake of humor, here it is. Have fun, break a few rules and let your humor fly free! We will go into some "rule-breaking" techniques in a later chapter.

Rule #7: Learn to laugh at yourself

Humorists need a tough skin. Why? Well, along with learning to laugh at life's situations, you have to learn to laugh at yourself. Don't be afraid to show off your weaknesses, mistakes or foibles. When you poke fun at yourself, you are allowing your audience to relate. I am the queen of the klutzy moves. I am still not allowed to handle a knife in my mother's house, and I am over 50 years old. I have a round face that would make the smile emoji jealous, and I have hair that makes Ronald McDonald's hair look tame. In other words, there is a lot of self-deprecating humor going on. BUT, and this is a big BUT, I don't write about this constantly. If you do nothing but poke fun at yourself, readers will view you as needy, whiny and will pity you instead of laugh at your attempt at humor. For example: I had a writer submit to HO three essays which all focused on her weight issues. The first one, I laughed at as who can't identify with the trials and tribulations of dieting, but by the middle of the second essay, I found myself no longer laughing at this woman but feeling sorry for her. By essay three, I was completely depressed and ate a sleeve of Girl Scout Thin Mint cookies. So make fun of yourself and your quirks and your life situations, but do not "weigh down" your readers with your troubles—be they dieting, medical issues, criminal investigations…well, you get it. Leave some mystery.

Some writers tell me they have no family or friends to use for their humor. The people in their lives want no part of their writing dreams. No biggie. Why not go the fictional route? I know humorists who make up family members, friends, co-workers, pets and their own personas just to avoid the potential problems that might evolve when writing about the real people in their lives. Humor always stretches the truth a bit, but some close to home might not accept that. So, if divorcing your real family and adopting a fake one helps you be a better humorist, go for it.

Rule #8: Start Writing

You will never know if you can swim if you don't get into the water. Let's have some fun and start writing.

Write for yourself. Each day write something—anything. Keep a journal, create a blog (Part II of this book), do whatever it takes to develop the discipline to write at least once a day. You don't have to be perfect; just get used to the idea of writing daily. Once you commit to this idea, writing becomes less intimidating and more enjoyable.

Writing Exercise:

   Write down memories of past embarrassing moments and see if you can turn mortification into mirth.

CHAPTER IV: The Formula Please?

During my journalist years, I interviewed a romance writer who lived not far from me. By day, she was a van-driving, girl scout-leading, soccer mom who was married to a plumber, but by night she morphed into this sultry vixen who wrote novels that I'm sure would make the readers of *50 Shades of Grey* blush. I remember being in awe of this mild-mannered woman—who lived in Lancaster County—yes, the Amish Country—and her ability to pen the steamy scenes that made her books popular with her fellow housewives and their husbands as well.

"It's all about the formula," she told me. "The publisher gives me a plan, and I know that on page 236, I have to insert a sex scene that hits certain criteria. I know when I have to talk about the first kiss, the foreplay, the actual sex act, etc. The formula is the reason I can turn out five novels per year."

The romance novelist's words were not a revelation to me. I knew writing formulas existed because magazines used them as well. Before I would query any magazine, I would study their articles to see what formula they followed. I would analyze the lead paragraphs and count how many paragraphs there were before the first quote appeared—these were their "tells." When I got down their formula, I knew I would be successful when submitting a query or article "on spec," and I knew I would get future assignments.

But to be honest, humor is a bit different. Sure, there are certain humor helpers that writers can use to draw in their readers, but is there a formula?

No. There is no formula. Well, that was blunt—but true—sort of. We all know humor when we read it or hear it, but to create it can prove to be a daunting task. Many novice humorists fall into the trap where they assume that each line of their essays or articles has to drip with non-stop funny. They believe that if their readers haven't died of a coronary from laughing too hard, they have failed in their attempt to be a humorist. To this I say, "Phooey!" Yes, I know this is a strong word, but I have reasons for this outburst. Here is what I say to both new humorists who are looking for the big laugh or to non-humorist writers who are hoping to add levity to an otherwise dry or tension-filled topic.

Your Writing Should Reflect Your Sense of Humor. In other words, be true to you. Do you like subtle or reserved humor? Do you like one-liners? Do you like wordplay? What makes you laugh? Writing humor should not be torture. It should be fun. I know that sounds simplistic, but it's the truth. In this chapter, we are going to explore some of the most common humor helpers. You can use one of the helpers or all of them. That's up to the humorist who lives within your soul. I need to extend a caveat here. You will see that I am big on caveats. These "tricks" are helpers and should not overshadow the integrity of the work. Yes, humor writing possesses integrity. Let the humor helpers enhance your creativity but not be your creativity. (So deep—right?)

Humor Helpers

When you read humor from different writers, you will see that each writer sets the pace for an essay or story. Some writers get right to the laughs and continue the jokes non-stop throughout the piece. You can feel the frenzy. Other writers meander through their story. They deliver subtle bits of humor that entertain you. Sometimes you laugh out loud and at other points in the story you simply smile. There are humorists who are experts at the element of surprise. They lull you into a calm and then blast you with the "funny" when you least expect it. As the writer, you want to set the pace and surprise your reader. How do you do this?

Sentence Length: Do you want your essay timing to be quick and emphatic? Short and to-the-point sentences might be ideal. Do you want your reader to feel the exasperation, fear or futility of an experience or situation? If that's the case, maybe you need long complex sentences where readers can barely take a breath because they are reliving your experience through your words. Use punctuation helpers like the em-dash (--) or the ellipsis (...) to identify a distinct pause or show hesitation, confusion, etc. Play with sentence length, but do not be afraid to vary it as your story or essay progresses. Sentence length will help reflect your emotion.

Punctuation: Most of the punctuation rules apply in humor, but some writers tend to rely on exclamation points to get the emotion across to the reader. STOP THAT!! Oops, I did it too—and doubled it! Seriously, use exclamation points sparingly. Rely on your storytelling ability to convey emotion.

Verb Voice: USE ACTIVE VOICE WHENEVER POSSIBLE. Active voice harnesses the energy of a piece. It allows readers to be the co-pilot in the adventure. Are there times when the writer needs to use passive voice? Yep, especially in humor, so don't beat yourself up if you bring in passive voice once in a while. But find those verbs that represent what it is you want to convey to your reader. I use an old-fashioned tool known as a thesaurus. Don't have a paperback copy? Find one online and consult it often. Another caveat: Don't pick out words from the thesaurus you would never use in your daily life. Writing humor should not turn into a vocabulary contest or a rehearsal for the SATs. Change up your wording without giving up your voice.

Adjectives and Adverbs: I like adjectives far better than adverbs. Adverbs offer quick clarity, but they are a cheap writing tool. Stick to action verbs and descriptive language and leave the adverbs out unless absolutely necessary. See, I used *absolutely*, but I thought it necessary. If you use an adverb, don't panic. There is no need to jump off a bridge in shame as some grammarians might suggest. Adverbs do exist for a reason, so if you need one, use it.

Alliteration: Alliteration is the repetition of initial consonant sounds in two or more neighboring words. Alliteration enhances humor whether it's used in a title or in the middle of an essay. Alliteration holds great power, but if it's overused, it will distract your reader and kill the funny.

> EXAMPLES:
> Similar Sounds Spark a Sense of Silliness.
> the Perturbed and Peeved Parent

Similes and Metaphors: A Simile is a figure of speech where two dissimilar things are compared with the help of words such as "like" or "as." I'll just jump into the example here as the definition is sort of boring.

> EXAMPLES:
> Her cheeks were red like a rose.
> His ego was as fragile as a plate of glass on the back of a pickup truck.
> She was as shallow as a kiddie pool.

A metaphor is a figure of speech that makes a less obvious comparison between two things that are unrelated.

> EXAMPLES:
> He is the black sheep of the family.
> Her confession was music to my ears.

Make it Bigger or Exaggerate: To put it simply, exaggeration overstates a situation, and it is a wonderful descriptive tool. One caveat for exaggeration: If your entire humor piece is exaggeration, your reader won't be able to tell truth from fiction and your piece loses all validity, and that's not a good idea if a writer is trying to relate a real-life experience. So use this humor helper, but use it wisely.

I loved using exaggeration in the following real-life happening when a squirrel decided to come indoors. Everything that occurred is true. I still cannot be sure if I exaggerated in the column or if I exaggerated in real life while this was going on. I'm pretty sure I still suffer from PTSQD or Post-Traumatic Squirrel Disorder. Here is an excerpt from "The Day of the Squirrel" when I trapped the rodent in my daughter's playroom.

EXAMPLE:

The squirrel crouched in the corner and shook with fear. Personally, I think it was overwhelmed by the hot pink paint, the Barbie border and the thousand or so naked dolls strewn around the room. If I were that small, I know this room would frighten the hell out of me. Amazingly, I came to my senses and slammed the door shut trapping the rodent inside. Then I made plans.

I called my husband at work to calmly tell him of the situation. I thought I was doing pretty well. His voicemail came on and what I planned to say was,

"We have a squirrel in the house; what do you think is the correct procedure?" What came out was,

"Where the hell are you? Why aren't you ever at your damn desk? Get home! There's a huge rodent in the Barbie room and it's chewing the heads off all the dolls!"

With that task done, I hung up. I then tried his cell number. Voicemail again. So, I left another well-thought-out message. In the meantime, I called exterminator after exterminator. Very few handle squirrels. Finally, one nice guy answered the phone, and I said,

"Help me. I have a squirrel trapped in my bedroom, please come now."

The man must have sensed the panic in my voice. He took my address and told me he'd be there as soon as possible—in about an hour and a half.

I don't think I need to mention that it was a long ninety minutes. When the exterminator did arrive, I met him at the door–still carrying my rake, of course. We crept up into the hallway and prepared to fling open the door. We assumed "Starsky and Hutch" positions. I thought we should call for back up, but he assured me he could handle the perpetrator himself. He went in and shut the door behind him. I heard furniture move, and I thought that the rabid rodent was eating him for lunch. But within a minute he came out and announced he didn't find the squirrel. Instead, he showed me a stuffed mermaid doll and said,

"This is probably what you saw."

"I don't think so," I chuckled politely while tightening the grip on my rake. "Come see the damage to my three-week-old, garden bay window."
from Life On The Off Ramp, Donna Cavanagh, 2010

Daffynitions: A combination of the words *daffy* and *definition*, a daffynition is a humorous and often twisted definition of an English word. These definitions can be puns or a twisted meaning of a common word.

EXAMPLES:
Legend – where the foot begins
Porcupine – when you crave sausage or bacon
Avoidable – what a bullfighter tries to do
Cannibal- someone who is fed up with people

The Rule of Three: I love the Rule of Three. It is easy, fun and provides an unseen ending to a good humor piece. How does it work? Well, in the traditional strategy, the writer sets up a premise and pretends to support the premise with three related ideas. Here's the twist: the first two ideas do support the premise, but the third idea adds an unexpected humorous end that catches the reader off guard which causes him or her to laugh (hopefully).

EXAMPLE:

The Mysterious Woman of Mars

The internet is all in a tizzy over the mysterious photo NASA received from Mars. The image in question shows what UFO experts (the experts who think aliens created the pyramids and Donald Trump) say is a long-haired woman walking upon the rocks on the red planet.
Scientists have presented three theories of their own and believe the figure is most likely one of the following:
1. Dust on the lens of the Mars camera
2. Light reflecting off a rock formation
or
3. Amelia Earhart

Donna Cavanagh, Humoroutcasts.com

There is an alternate Rule of Three as well. It's not considered a true humor tool, but in my book it packs as big a punch. In this

Rules of Three, each item in the list has a humorous feel and builds to the final twisted punch line.

EXAMPLE:

The End of Men

Scientists have determined that the Y chromosome will die out in five million years and men will become extinct. What does this mean for the future of the world?
1. Toilet seats will no longer be made to flip up.
2. The Catholic Church will finally ordain women as priests.
3. Lesbians, lesbians, lesbians.

Donna Cavanagh, Humoroutcasts.com

Sarcasm: We all know sarcasm when we hear it, but can we write it? In its definition, sarcasm is a humorous remark that on the surface seems to be complimenting someone but in truth it is criticizing or cutting someone down. When done right, sarcasm can be a great literary device, but sarcasm can be interpreted as mean-spirited, so use caution as to the amount of sarcasm you use in one particular piece.

EXAMPLES:
Those cooking classes really paid off. (This is not sarcasm if the meal is good, but if you are running to the bathroom after one bite, I would think sarcasm.)
Stuffing your face with those doughnuts is a great way to train for the marathon.

Irony: The use of words to express the opposite of the literal meaning of the real meaning. Irony can be a close companion of sarcasm.

> **EXAMPLES:**
> That was a nice surprise! (It is nice if you got a big bouquet of roses, but if you come home to your home being burglarized—well, that is an ironic statement.)
> My neighbors have a three-pound teacup terrier named Killer.
> Breaking News: A committed vegan got attacked by a runaway cow.
> The new Weight Watchers site is next to the Doughnut Shop, Chinese Take-out and pizza parlor in the new shopping center. Well, that might not be irony as much as good marketing. But you get my point.

Making Lists: To me, lists are the big brother of the Rules of Three. List building allows you to build momentum and come in for the "kill" at the end of a piece or it allows the writer to keep a constant wave of laughter throughout an essay. Lists can be phrases or short sentences or they can be mini-stories in their own right. Today's readers love brevity, and the lists allow a writer to pen a longer piece while delivering short spurts of information throughout the essay that keep a reader's attention. In other words, lists not only engage readers, keep their minds focused on the work.

EXAMPLE:

How to Avoid Ghosts and Other Paranormal Fun

Last night while flipping through the channels, I came upon the show Celebrity Ghost Stories. I have to say Hollywood's stars have some pretty creepy experiences to share.

During this episode, I watched Christopher Knight, Margaret Cho and some unfamiliar actress tell their real-life ghostly encounters. Are these things real? Sure, why not? Who am I to judge? I plan on coming back and wreaking havoc on unsuspecting living people. Why? Because I can and there are some people who I would like to drive to the brink of insanity—I think it would be fun.

Personally, I think ghosts are okay guests as long as they are not ghosts who insist on taking over the house or the person living in the house as was the case with the unfriendly demons in The Exorcist or Amityville Horror. The celebrity ghostly encounters got me thinking about house hauntings, so I have come up with a few rules which should help both celebrities and regular people avoid paranormal and possession mayhem.

Don't move into a house with a history *- By history I mean "crime" history. Murder, suicide—anything violent is a sign that this house might not be for you. Okay, say the seller forgets to disclose the fact that six people were murdered in the house, and you move in only to discover that a few weeks down the road, your five-year-old kid drops the F-bomb constantly while his head makes 360-degree spins. Should you be alarmed?*

Yes, you should be very alarmed, and you need to leave. This is my problem with these shows. People stay in houses even after a once sweet spouse grows horns on his or her head and displays glowing red eyes which were once baby blue. They blame the demon transformation on everything from the weather to eating bad fish. I am as skeptical as the next person, but if you are alone in a room and a loud and angry voice yells, "GET OUT!" do yourself a favor and get out! Get out as fast as your little feet can take you. Those stupid Amityville people waited until blood started to stream down the walls and for the husband to turn homicidal before they abandoned ship. Here's a rule of thumb: If your spouse is coming at you with a hatchet, you might have waited too long.

Don't move into a house or apartment where the rent should be $4000 a month but the landlord charges you $200 per month - *Let me just say this straight out: No one wants to give you a great deal on rent because you are special. You are not that special—no one is. A really good deal on rent is obviously a sign that the apartment was a site for satanic worship. I learned this fact from watching Rosemary's Baby. If someone wants you to lease an apartment that badly, something is definitely wrong. That eighty-plus-percent rent discount (I don't know if that is the right percentage as I suck at math so all you engineers can figure that out for me) is not because there is a roach or rodent problem. No, that big discount should be a red flag—a warning that you will be sharing that apartment with someone who is not of this world.*

Do not buy a home that has had ten owners in the past year - *If a house spits out owners this fast, there is a problem. And while I think that owners are legally supposed to disclose all problems with the house, they tend to fib a bit when it comes to ghosts. I guess since not everyone believes in ghosts, one can blame any unexplainable happenings on old plumbing or the house settling.*

Don't buy a house that is next to a cemetery or was once a funeral home - *I had a friend in high school who lived above her father's funeral parlor which she now owns herself. Did she have ghostly experiences? Yes, and she told us amazing stories, but they were all benign in nature. There were no mean ghosts who threw things around the room. Mostly, she said the ghosts commented on their funerals and what their families made them wear.*

However, I saw that movie A Haunting in Connecticut and its television version that was on that show A Haunting. In the story a family unknowingly moves into an old funeral home. While a Twitter friend, who wrote the book for this paranormal story, has said publicly that this entire story was a hoax, I have to believe it is still best not to live in an old funeral home. Okay, let me amend that. It's okay to live in an old funeral home but unlike the people in this tale, do the smart thing and remove the embalming equipment from the basement before you make it a bedroom for your young sons, and here is another tip: don't use the freezer that once housed the cadavers as a place to store your groceries. Get a new freezer; Life will be much easier.

Donna Cavanagh, Humoroutcasts.com

There once was a girl from Nantucket or Poetry for Humor:

Would you like poetry if it was not serious, symbolic or deep? Do you care about iambic pentameter? Do you know what iambic pentameter is? If not, you can be a humor poet. Yes, humor poetry is a real thing and if written well, you will probably make more money than those boring poets who write about nature, love and lofty ideals. Is rhyming easy? No. But with a little practice, you too can bring a new dimension to your funny world. Sure, you might insult a few people here and there and damage a literary genre that has been around since the dawn of civilization, but that's humor.

EXAMPLE:

Some write poems filled with emotion
Some write poems filled with pain
When a humorist comes up with a crazy notion
She can write about food, sex or Chow Mein

No symbolism is required to make people smile

No poetic rules can keep creativity bound
Sure the poetic elite might groan for a while
But some funny rhyming might also astound

(I have no publishing reference for this one. I made this up just for you. Same thing for the Haiku above)

Haiku – The three-line joke?

Some writers love haikus. Honestly, I'm not a big fan because I get way too frustrated trying to fit everything I want to say in five syllables, seven syllables and five syllables. I am more of a 144-syllable-236-syllable-416-syllable kind of gal. But for the sake of fairness, let's embrace the haiku.

> EXAMPLE:
>   The fly buzzed near me
>   I swat it with my cellphone.
>   Fly lives; iPhone dies

Show Off Your Pun: A pun is a humorous substitution of words that are similar in sound but not in meaning. Puns are an old form of humor, but their use never gets old. They make us groan out loud, but both readers and writers delight in a good pun. Non-humorists like to insert puns into speeches or writing to bring some levity to more serious topics. Puns are excellent for tension tamers. I offer you pun EXAMPLES from a man I consider the "King of Puns" Bill Spencer.

EXAMPLES:
If you've seen ONE bear attack movie, you've seen a maul.

At least this pooch didn't get up on your Bark-alounger.

Once, MY imaginary dog got up on the dining room table, and when I told him to "Get down!" he started dancing.

My imaginary dog could read. He saw a sign on a park bench that said "Wet Paint," and he did. Sadly, he died after eating a whole can of varnish. It was a terrible end. A terrible end. But a beautiful finish.
Bill Spencer, HumorOutcasts writer

Misdirection: A simple statement whereby readers think the writer is taking them down a certain path only to find out they have not only been re-routed but thrown off the road.

EXAMPLE:
The basis of this misdirection EXAMPLE came from a true news story. It's short and throws the reader off the track for the ending.

Domino's Delivers

A man claimed he had sex with a Domino's pizza and as a result he burnt his penis. I am appalled and shocked. My Domino's pizzas are usually cold by the time they get to my house.
Donna Cavanagh, Humoroutcasts.com

Most readers were groaning about the burnt penis, but cold pizza can be a problem too.

Dialogue: Dialogue makes me crack up. There is something about the conversation between two people or perhaps an imaginary conversation in someone's head that ignites laughter. It doesn't have to take up the entire essay or be a long conversation, but it needs to convey the correct emotion of the essay.

EXAMPLE:

The Literary Elite at Starbucks

I decided I needed a quick pick-me-up, so I headed to Starbucks. I was sitting with my coffee and crossword puzzle at a table in the corner when I started to eavesdrop on the conversation between the two people at the tables next to mine. Technically, it was not eavesdropping as they were both talking pretty loudly, and their conversation was hard to avoid. Both of these people had a laptop in front of them, and each was supposedly busy creating the next great novel or movie or whatever.

I have to admit that right away I got intimidated. I know that sounds silly, but people who write in public on laptops just do that to me. They seem so artsy and sure of themselves. It's not that I can't write in public. I was a reporter, so I had to learn to write in the most unusual places such as the state penitentiary for men. I always say if you can write a story and make a deadline during a prison lockdown, you can write anywhere.

I should explain that I didn't go to the prison because I liked the creative atmosphere. The prison was part of my beat, so I had an obligation to go there at least once a week. Every once in a while there was a security problem that resulted in a lockdown and my spending more time in the prison than anticipated. For all of the inmates who might have been paroled since my last visit, I just want to say that I am NOT making fun of you or your confinement here, and I wish to thank you for all the kind compliments about my appearance you gave me through the years of your unfortunate incarceration.

Anyway, back to the Starbucks writers. They started to discuss dialogue and plot development and blah, blah, blah, and I started to think how boring my writing was. They were talking about creating literature while my last freelance assignment was writing about the vampire craze and how it affects the retail world. It's easy to see why I would think my work lacks excitement although I did get an invitation from a California store owner who asked me to come to her store to witness firsthand a blood-drinking ceremony.

As I sat at my table pretending to do my puzzle, I started to wonder how these writers got work done surrounded by so much pastry. If I did my writing in a Starbucks, I would be 400 pounds. No, I would be 400 pounds and unpublished because all I would do is eat the baked goods.

As I continued to listen to their conversation, the "What Kind of Writer Are You?" drama started to play in my head. Most writers have some kind of individual drama that plays inside their brains on occasion. Mine usually does a matinee and evening performance on a daily basis. This is how it can go:

Insane self: "You are a waste of a writer. Look how boring your assignments are! These people are creating literature.

Sane self: "Shut up! I can write! I have tons of publishing credits to my name too."

Insane self: "Yes, but who wants to read your books? They will never be featured on Oprah's Book Club!"

Sane self: "I don't need Oprah! Wait... did I just say that? I'm sorry, Oprah. I'm so sorry. I do need you! Don't be mad at me! Come back, Oprah! Oh God, I think I need to switch to decaf."

Donna Cavanagh, Try and Avoid the Speed Bumps (HumorOutcasts Press, 2012)

The dialogue was not extensive, but if any dialogue can show how crazy I can be, this is it. How could one cup of coffee at Starbucks turn into a complete meltdown?

Writing Exercise:

Choose a topic from the news and find a humorous angle for that topic. Add dialogue or descriptions using puns or exaggeration. How does adding humor helpers change the emotion of the story or the focus?

_____

_____

_____

_____

_____

_____

_____

CHAPTER V: Putting Together an Essay

Do you know the number one challenge facing humorists today? Take a guess. Is it political correctness? Buzz…wrong answer. If that was your response, go back to Chapter I and re-read the part about how political correctness and humor don't mix. Is the number one challenge, lack of ideas? Probably not. The number one challenge…drum roll please…word count.

"How can that be, oh author of this totally untextbook-like humor book?"

Well, let me explain, oh students eager to learn.

Many years ago, there was this thing called print media. It was wonderful. Each day, people all over the world would go outside to their front lawns and pick up this rolled-up package called a newspaper, and inside that newspaper there were long articles and wonderful information and coupons. Okay, there are still coupons, but so many of the long articles are gone. The culprit for the extinction of long articles: the internet.

No, I am not going to bash the internet as I cannot function without it. However, there is a downside. We get much information and entertainment so quickly that speed has become our normal existence. And because we embrace speed, our attention spans have decreased dramatically. I read an article a few years back about a Canadian study that determined human beings now have a shorter attention span than goldfish.

I'm no goldfish expert. I know when it's time to flush them, but the idea that they can focus longer than humans is sort of scary. What does that mean for humorists? It means that an essay that once counted 1,200 words now should be no more than 700 words. To counteract the nanoseconds-of-reader-interest problem, many writers employ the use of photos and short videos to deliver their humor instead of words. In a visual and fast world, why not?

I don't mean to scare away the long-winded writers. There are definitely exceptions to the short-and-fast philosophy. Every once in a while, I have to hit the 800-word count. When I break the brevity rule and go long, I do so because I believe abbreviating the essay would compromise the quality of that essay.

It takes a bit of practice to cut down an essay and select the words that will deliver your humor punch, but you can learn to do it. You want to be the one in control of what gets cut out of your essay. Don't leave it in the hands of an editor who might not get your humor or what you are trying to convey to the reader.

Now that we understand how important word count can be and the need to pick your words, let's look at what it takes to write an essay.

Essay writing is a great place for a budding humorist to start. Unlike short stories and novels, essays do not involve plot building, character development or story continuity. It's up to 700 words of literary fun. So what do you need to worry about when writing a humor essay?

For me, writing an essay is like building an ice cream sundae. You start with the basics or your favorite flavor which for the essay is the topic. Next, you pile on the fudge or peanut butter sauce which is your hook. (If ice cream isn't your thing, build a pizza. I have a sweet tooth.) The hook is going to grab your readers and make them want to go further into the essay. Then you add the whipped cream, sprinkles or nuts. These sundae extras are the humor helpers you use to bring your essay to life and finally, and the all-important maraschino cherry is your perfect conclusion. (It's good to know that even if I teach you nothing about humor in this book, you now know how to create one heck of an ice cream masterpiece.)

For this chapter, I am going to dissect one of my most read essays *The Umpire's Wife Has Been Ejected*. We are going to break it down by topic, hook, body and conclusion. Then we can look at it in one piece to illustrate how it all works. But first let's look at the components for an essay.

The Topic: If you did any of the exercises in the previous pages of this book, you have explored some of the resources for a good topic. In case you haven't done any of the exercises yet, I'll give you some ideas for topics.

Marriage and relationships
Children
Pets
School
Friends
Politics
Religion
Sex

Notice that I did not add work or office into that mix. Why? These are tricky topics. People have been fired for posting on Facebook, so if you are going to poke fun at your office, boss or corporation, you better be independently wealthy, pretty sure you can find another job quickly or work in an environment that welcomes humor. The business world has a short fuse when it comes to humor. Don't burn yourself over a joke.

While we are on the subject of caution, always think twice about the repercussions that go along with certain topics like religion and politics. As I said before, humor is an important tool to get people to think. However, this is a volatile world where extremism can be dangerous. Humorists need to understand that dangers exist and because humor is subjective, not everyone will find your humor enchanting. With those words of caution out of the way, let's build an essay.

"The Umpire's Wife Has Been Ejected" by Donna Cavanagh (Referee magazine, July 2011)

Essay topic: umpire husband throws wife out of game (marriage and relationships)

The Hook: A hook is like a magnet, and your reader should be pulled in and not able to let go. The first sentence of an essay should show the reader where they think the story or essay is going. There might be twists and turns before the essay is over, but the reader has a direction. In a humor essay, the first paragraph should never be serious. You don't have to generate belly-rolling laughs, but a reader should be sensing the humor to come.

My husband has umpired for baseball and softball for about 10 years. Some umpire wives go to games to see their husbands in action. Me, I rarely attend. It's not that I am not interested. I don't go because I don't want to be ejected again.

By the end of the first paragraph, the reader knows there will be trouble. Now the questions start. Did he truly eject his own wife? (Yes.) What could she have done to earn such punishment? (A lot.) Are they still married? (Yes.)

The Body: The action of the essay. It can be more than a paragraph, and you can employ any or none of the humor helpers we discussed earlier. As a writer, you might be telling a straight story with humor throughout or using these paragraphs to set up readers to surprise them. It all depends where your story is going. In my essay, I started out on the tame side, but I used the humor helpers to illustrate the building tension which led to my husband ejecting me from the field. Notice that I did use alliteration, repetition and some long and complex sentences to help depict how the situation was getting out of hand.

Yes, in one of his rare ejections, my husband tossed me from the field of play. I will admit that he had no choice. At this game, which in our house is forever known as the "the night we almost got

- 46 -

divorced" game, my husband was the home plate ump for a 14-and-under fastpitch softball game which decided which team got to go to Nationals. At this game, where he ejected me (in case you didn't read that part), I stopped by the field to bring him an extra drink. I stood near the bleachers that were next to the first base line. There were already two outs in the inning, and I felt some tension from the crowd sitting in those bleachers. After the batter took the first pitch, the ump let out a loud "Strike." Then I heard a father in the bleachers scream,

"Are you blind? Are you an idiot? That was clearly a ball."

Ah, the sound of a perturbed and peeved parent. It's a sad fact of organized sports that each team has one of those parents who cannot keep his or her mouth shut. These parents feel it is their right to try and sway, through intimidation, the way an umpire calls a game.

Back to this game – you know the one where my husband ejected me – Did I mention that already? I knew I should have left when I realized that there was a troublemaker parent in the vicinity, but like a good train wreck, I had to stick around and watch. The irate dad was upset at everything from the balls and strikes calls to how the third-base coach was telling his base runners to lead. After the second pitch, my husband called another strike. The irate parent barked louder. Finally, the batter swung and missed the last pitch, which ended the inning.

Well, it ended the inning for everyone but the father of the kid who struck out. He continued to scream. My husband looked at the coach, who yelled at the parent who cursed at my husband.

That's when I got involved. I told him that he was an embarrassment and that this game was supposed to teach kids about sportsmanship. Now the coach and the other parents chimed in. They were yelling at this dad, and I was yelling at this dad, and he was yelling at me, and then my husband came over and glared at me and the dad, and he ejected us both. Shocked, I stormed off the field. However, I did realize that I did not help the situation. In my defense, I think the crowd was happy I came to the game because I gave the ump a good excuse to get rid of the parent from hell.

The Conclusion: I like conclusions in my essays. I don't like to keep my readers hanging. Often, I will end an essay with something like "What can we learn from this...?" and set up a Rule of Three and take the essay through another twist. My favorite ending is the circle. Honestly, I don't know what the true terminology is for this "trick," but I like my ending language to make a U-turn to the beginning of the essay. To me, it gives the reader the sense that the story is complete. In our EXAMPLE essay, I used puns to direct back to the umpire theme that started the initial story.

When my husband got home that night, I was still mildly miffed. He apologized, but he said I left him no choice. "I probably would have ejected that guy in the next inning anyway," he confessed. "I give parents time to think. It's best for the kids if they don't see their parents ejected."

I forgave him, and then the ump thought we were back to normal, so he tried to circle the bases at home with me. Silly, silly ump. It was my turn to eject him from the playing field.

And the essay in full form:

The Umpire's Wife Has Been Ejected

My husband has been a baseball and softball umpire for about 10 years. Some umpire wives go to games to see their husbands ump. Me, I rarely attend. It's not that I am not interested. I don't want to be ejected again.

Yes, in one of his rare ejections, my husband tossed me from the field of play. I will admit that he had no choice. At this game, which in our house is forever known as the "the night we almost got divorced" game, my husband was the home plate ump for a 14-and-under fastpitch softball game which decided which team got to go to Nationals. At this game, where he ejected me (in case you didn't read that part), I stopped by the field to bring him an extra drink. I stood near the bleachers that were next to the first-base line. There were already two outs in the inning, and I felt some tension from the

- 48 -

crowd sitting in those bleachers. After the batter took the first pitch, the ump let out a loud "Strike." Then I heard a father in the bleachers scream,

"Are you blind? Are you an idiot? That was clearly a ball."

Ah, the sound of a perturbed and peeved parent. It's a sad fact of organized sports that each team has one of those parents who cannot keep his or her mouth shut. These parents feel it is their right to try and sway, through intimidation, the way an umpire calls a game.

Back to this game – you know the one where my husband ejected me – Did I mention that already? I knew I should have left when I realized that there was a troublemaker parent in the vicinity, but like a good train wreck, I had to stick around and watch. The irate dad was upset at everything from the balls and strikes calls to how the third-base coach was telling his base runners to lead. After the second pitch, my husband called another strike. The irate parent barked louder. Finally, the batter swung and missed the last pitch, which ended the inning.

Well, it ended the inning for everyone but the father of the kid who struck out. He continued to scream. My husband looked at the coach, who yelled at the parent who cursed at my husband.

That's when I got involved. I told him that he was an embarrassment and that this game was supposed to teach kids about sportsmanship. Now, the coach and the other parents chimed in. They were yelling at this dad, and I was yelling at this dad, and he was yelling at me, and then my husband came over and glared at me and the dad, and he ejected us both. Shocked, I stormed off the field. However, I did realize that I did not help the situation. In my defense, I think the crowd was happy I came because I gave the ump a good excuse to get rid of the parent from hell.

When my husband got home that night, I was still mildly miffed. He apologized, but he said I left him no choice. "I probably would have ejected that guy in the next inning anyway," he confessed. "I give parents time to think. It's best for the kids if they don't see their parents ejected." I forgave him, and then the ump thought we were back to normal, so he tried to circle the bases at home with me. Silly, silly ump. It was my turn to eject him from the playing field.

Referee magazine, July 2011

This essay worked for me and a lot of different readers too. Two magazines picked it up, so the topic resonated with people. However, there is always a chance that an idea falters or can't get off the ground. So what do you do? How long do you stick by the idea? When do you move on?

When an idea falters: There is no clear-cut time limit for working on an idea to see if it works or not. Each humorist must maintain his or her own writing rules. My rule is twenty minutes. I know that makes me seem like the most impatient person in the world, but I've been at this almost thirty years. If I don't have an essay complete in those twenty minutes, I pretty much know it's not going to happen. Sometimes I discard the idea completely; other times I file it away in case inspiration hits at a later date.

Upon hearing my twenty-minute rule, one aspiring writer in a workshop commented, "Determination must not be in your blood." To which I replied in a most polite manner, "Don't confuse determination with obsession. There is a difference between forging ahead and beating a dead horse." (I mean that figuratively and in case anyone is offended please note that no animals were harmed or killed in the making of this how-to-write humor book.)

Let's keep it simple and say this: It's okay for an idea not to work out and to put that idea aside because letting go allows a writer to open up his or her mind to new inspiration and creativity, and that is when the spark ignites.

Editing your essay: Always edit your work. Read it out loud and then look for spelling and typos. Reading aloud helps a writer feel the humor. I make most changes after I hear an essay. I hear what words I want to emphasize and also hear where I want pauses to be or where I want the emotion to change.

I have another caveat. In recent years, the trend for editing is to do away with commas. I asked an editor friend about this, and her response was that modern-day editors don't know how to incorporate commas into the written word, so they made it trendy to eliminate them. I don't know if this is totally true, but I still say "UGHHHHHH!" I like commas and what they represent. I continue to use them. My rule for comma usage: be consistent. That's all I got on the comma conundrum except to say it's so sad to think that a good punctuation mark is on the outs with the literary world.

Writing Exercise:

Try out a humor essay. Use your topic from the previous exercise. Create a hook around the topic and add a few sentences for the body. Try using one or two humor helpers and brainstorm a conclusion. The essay does not have to be perfect. You can go back and add to or subtract from it, but **DO THE ESSAY!**

_____

_____

_____

_____

_____

_____

_____

PART II: HOW DO I GET MY WORK OUT THERE?

The second part of this book is aimed at the true novice writer who has not yet explored the world of online publication. However, there are many experienced writers out there who feel intimidated by the internet. Use this book to rid yourself of that fear. The internet is a mysterious place, but it can be a fun place to hang out and find readers for your work. On the discussion block are blogging, both individual blogs and community blogs, the importance of social media and online etiquette. Yes, believe it or not, manners count!

CHAPTER VI: Blogging, Books and Beyond

A show of hands: Who remembers the days when you would send a pitch letter or query to a magazine editor and then wait anxiously six to eight weeks for a response? If you do remember this process, give yourself a round of applause because you have paid your writing dues more than most.

Today's writing world is such a different animal from the "pre-internet" days. Back in olden times, rejection letters held no shame. I, myself, would tape them up onto my office wall and use them as inspiration to become a better writer. I will admit that some of these letters, which came via snail mail, made me chuckle. My favorite was from an editor who wrote to tell me he was going to call me so he could tell me via phone why my essay stunk. Yes, apparently shooting me down through the US Post Office was not sufficient. To be fair to this man, he did indeed call, and he rejected me because he considered humor to be nothing but a mixture of "fluff and stupid," and he was disappointed that a former journalist would debase herself by writing such unimportant material.

Now, some people might have become upset by that rejection, but not me. I entered this experience into a contest whose theme was "WORST REJECTION LETTER EVER," and I won second place. I cannot even imagine who won the top prize. I didn't win money, but I did win a t-shirt screen printed with the words "Rejected Writer." Yep, that is the God's honest truth. If I sponsored that contest, I would have taken a more optimistic approach and sent out a t-shirt that read "Amazing Writer in Progress," but I'm a glass-half-full person.

The world of writing is not all about rejection. However, if you contemplate jumping off a bridge each time you do get rejected, I would suggest you pursue another line of work or hobby. I will admit that there is no better feeling than having an editor tell you that your article or essay has been accepted. That is a champagne-popping moment. And it makes all the rejections seem so not important.

Even today, I still get rejection letters or emails. They don't faze me anymore. It's part of the game in my view. And truth be told, I deliver rejections now. HumorOutcasts.com is a submission acceptance site. I or Betsy—and if you don't know the truth about Betsy, go back to the introduction—audition writers and their work. The reason for this is that I promote HO writers extensively, and I cannot do that if I allow everyone to post. I also think knowing a site is not a "gimme" inspires writers to bring their best work—or for those who enjoy sports metaphors—their "A" game.

I know some might deem the next part of this sentence as new-agey or a bit on the La-La side, but I think the Universe makes room for all writers. We might not all be bestselling authors or syndicated columnists on the Erma Bombeck scale, but our work does get seen. And the reason for this is that there is an audience for humor; people crave it, so let's do our best to get it out there, and now I want to show you how.

The first question I ask writers when they tell me they want to "put forth their work" is this: what do you hope to accomplish? Are you looking for money? Honestly, writing is not the best field for you if that is your number one answer. Most writers I know don't smell of cash; they barely smell of pennies. But it could happen. You could hit it big and write the humor version of *War and Peace.*

If money is not your thing, is it fame? I know many writers who believe they are going to rock Hollywood with their humor magic. Again, it might just happen. I am here to support dreams not deny them. The reason I ask writers about their goals is to guide them about what they can do to get their work noticed. There is NO right or wrong answer for what you want to gain from your writing. No one should ever judge your ambitions; they are yours and yours alone, and I say good for you and keep working toward them.

I know this section of the book is entitled "Blogging, Books and Beyond," but before I get into the blogging part, I want to tackle traditional print media and magazines. There are still wonderful publications out there although they are a lot thinner than they used to be, so getting picked up by them is more of a challenge. Some still look for outside writers for humorous true stories that fit their demographic. So, how do you get them to notice your work.

THE PITCH OR QUERY LETTER:

I don't think the query letter has changed much in the last twenty years except now most are emailed instead of snail mailed. Most editors like a shorter query too as these editors now hold more responsibility with smaller staffs to help them out. Despite the changes with magazines, editors have told me they still look for the same three points: the hook, followed by details of the essay or article including some facts or quotes and finally, a conclusion as to why a piece would fit with the publication. The query should also give the editor a preview of your writing style.

This is a query I did for my first humor column in *First* Magazine more than twenty years ago. The magazine is totally different now, so today this might not fly, but the structure of the query is a basic one and hasn't changed much. The query did its job. I not only sold the essay, but the magazine made me their primary humor columnist for about five years.

Dear (I found out the editor's name and addressed the query to her),

Two months ago I almost lost my family when we embarked on an adventure for which none of us were prepared: a yard sale. Yes, this seemingly banal event stirred within us feelings of distrust and horror as we decided which of our prized possessions would be tagged for sale.

"Why is there a $500 sticker on my T-bird," my husband screamed in panic.

"You have 2000 Barbies," I begged my daughter. "Let some of them go free."

"Okay, sell the microwave, but no more homemade dinners," I reminded my family.

Yard sales might be an American tradition, but I would surmise that many of your readers do not know the hidden dangers behind them. I would love to educate them with a 750-word column detailing these pitfalls so they can avoid the turmoil we experienced. With your demographic centered around 35-55-year-old females with children, I think this essay would resonate and provide a much needed break from the stress of everyday life or at the very least, the stress of planning a yard sale.

For your information, I am a multi-published humorist whose work has appeared in daily papers throughout Pennsylvania and national publications such as USA Today. I would be happy to send you some of my published columns. I look forward to your feedback, and I hope we can work together in the future.

Thank you,
Donna Cavanagh

I will be honest and say that I have not written a traditional query letter in more than a decade. As my readership grew, I got to know more editors who only required me to send them a few sentences about what I wanted to do. I still got rejections, and I still do. In the writing world, no one or nothing is a sure thing.

If you send out a query and get a positive response, you still need to do your homework about that publication. I suggest that you go to your local library and pull the last six issues of the magazine and study it. Study how the articles are structured. Study what they look for in a lead paragraph and when they bring in quotes and facts. By studying the articles, you will learn who their audience is. Never write without knowing about the demographic you are trying to entertain.

BLOGGING:

Okay, let's learn about the best writer's tool to come along ever: *The Blog.* The blog is a powerful platform for both "newbies" and experienced writers. A blog gives writers the opportunity to share their talent with the entire world.

I cannot imagine how much easier my writing life would have been if the blog had been around in the 1980s and early 1990s. I don't think a blog would have catapulted me to fame and fortune, but I do think it might have instilled in me the discipline to write each day hoping that with each post, I would gain another follower for my humor.

There are two types of blogs: the individual blog and the community blog. I am going to go through both and the pros and cons for them as well.

The Individual Blog: Remember a few pages back when I asked what are you hoping to accomplish with your writing? Well, this is why I asked. Some writers need to be the one and only focus of the blog. They want a reader not to be distracted by another writer's work, and they want a blog to reflect their own style of humor only. It's not about getting paid since individual bloggers don't get paid as a rule unless they find a way to pay themselves or a sponsor to pay them advertising. Another caveat: advertising sponsors are not keen on humor. It's difficult for them to embrace any written word that is not G-rated, and a lot of humor is not for all audiences. It makes them nervous that the Family Council or one of those other militant groups will call for a boycott of their products because they sponsor "bad taste" humor.

There is nothing selfish about wanting to be the star of the show, and, in fact, when writers are starting out or building an audience, they need that spotlight on them.

Starting a blog is not a difficult task. You can use a template service to create a blog. I don't want to give support to any specific platform in this book, so I encourage you to Google "create a blog," and you will have more than enough information at your fingertips.

Those who are not as tech-savvy might be more comfortable hiring a company to set up a blog complete with a banner and logo. These services will monitor your blog and update software as needed. The startup is often free, but eventually you will have to pay maintenance for the site. Read the fine print.

The Community Blog: A community blog is exactly what its name states. It is a site where numerous writers contribute their work. Some community sites pay some or all their writers, while others do not pay at all. Community sites publish a diversity of writers and types of humor so they tend to get more hits per day than an individual blog, but more hits for the site does not necessarily mean more exposure for each individual writer.

Why? Not all community sites promote each writer. The reason might be as simple as they are so well-known, they don't need to do anything extra to bring in reads. That's good for them, but not so good for the writer who is looking to build a fan base.

Let's go through the pros and cons of both types of blogs so you know what's ahead whether you choose to start an individual blog, join a community site or maybe do both. Yes, there is no rule that says you can't have your own blog and write for a larger blog site. When trying to get your work read, almost everything is fair.

The Pros of an Individual Blog:

- You are the star.
- There is always space for your work.
- No editors to reject your work.
- You can decide how often you want to post to your blog.
- Your blog is a great place to try out book ideas or test the waters on subject matter.
- Promotion is all up to you. Now that might sound like a negative, and it can be if you are not comfortable talking about yourself, but it's also a good thing as it gives you control over marketing strategy.
- You can join networks and link to individual bloggers like yourself. There are blogging groups on social media and sometimes even groups that meet in your area to talk about blogging. It's nice to have company!
- You can start to build a brand of your own.
- You can invite people to subscribe to your blog and create an email list so that when you post your work, you can blast the link out to that list and bring more people to your blog.

Cons of an Individual Blog:

- You are the star. (Yes, it cuts both ways.) If you do not provide sufficient content or content that your readers like, they will go elsewhere. Remember humor is subjective.
- Depending upon what blog guru you follow or read, the average individual blog gets between two and twelve hits per post. That number is not as important as

the fact that it takes a long time to build a following, so patience must be one of your greatest assets.

- Learn to like and use social media because if you don't, no one will know you have a blog. We are going to go into the more popular social media platforms in the next chapter.
- You have to be a conscientious blog manager. If you let your blog become stale, it will falter and die out. Understand your audience and post often to bring that audience back to your blog often.
- You will depend upon other single bloggers for support, and while you might prove to be a gem in the cooperation department, other bloggers might prove to be pretty stingy with cross-promotion. Sometimes this is a tough lesson to learn.
- Depending upon which stat you find, there are anywhere from 152 million to 172 million blogs in the world or more by the time this book comes out. The reason the number is hard to nail down is that many bloggers give up within weeks of starting their blogs, and while these blogs might officially still exist, they are sort of gathering dust in a small corner of the internet. Whatever the true number of blogs out there is, it's a lot and that's a lot of competition for reads.
- If you get discouraged or fall behind in your posting, you will become one of those inactive blogs, and if a reader comes to read your work and your last entry was more than a week before his or her previous visit, you probably will never see that reader again.

The Pros of a Community Blog:

- You don't shoulder the burden alone. You are one of ten or a hundred or a thousand writers. If you don't post, someone will. (You need to check the writer's guidelines for the community blog or talk to the editor to make sure there is no minimum posting requirement.)
- You have a built-in audience. Community blogs are already established with regular readers. It's an easy way to get your work seen by a fan base.
- There is a diversity of writers who write on various topics. It's a great place to comment and learn about other topics, and writing styles and maybe a nice place to ask for some constructive criticism too.
- Community blogs will invite you to spread your creative wings and push the envelope a bit.
- Posts on a community blog have a greater chance of being picked up by other online sites and media.
- A community blog might be agreeable about promoting your other writing projects such as your individual blog, books, videos and podcasts.

WRITER RESPONSIBILITY

Of course, with these advantages also comes some responsibility to the community site and your fellow writers, and the majority of your responsibility can be summed up in one sentence: **JUST BE NICE**.

- Promote your work and the work of others.

- Become a part of the community. Read and comment even on days you don't post.
- Don't Stop and Drop. Stop and Drop is when you post on a community blog and don't take the time to read other writers' work or comment on their posts. Stop and Stay and become part of that community. Community sites are great places to build relationships and friendships. If you stop and drop you prevent those relationships from building. Writing is a solitary profession. A community blog takes some of the loneliness away.
- Use social media not only for your sake as a writer but for the sake of potential readers as well. When you share humor posts, you deliver the gift of laughter. So many people need that in their lives.
- Do not form cliques. When I was on some of the larger internet sites, I sometimes thought I was back in high school. Cliques formed when writers would say, "If you click on my post, I'll click on yours and we can get more hits that way." Some sites paid per hit, so I understand their logic, but in the long run, writers who did this got a few more cents in their pockets but those clicks did not mean people read their work. Isn't the main point of writing to entertain and inform readers?
- Learn the rules of the site. Most sites have an FAQ section on their home page to address becoming a site author and author etiquette. If you are unsure of something, ask the administrator (admin) or the editor. There should be contact info on the site, and they will be grateful you took the time to ask.
- If you are going to promote your work from another site or promote your new book, make sure it's okay with the

editor or admin. It is common courtesy to check with them before you use them for free publicity. They might be thrilled to help, but still ask.

- Feel free to promote your work that is published on a community site. However, if you post the same essay or article on a number of different sites, don't promote all the links at once.
- If you decide to leave a community site that has helped you, let the editors know. An editor who is committed to helping writers will be happy that a writer found a better fit for his or her work outside their blog. It never pays to burn bridges.

SITE RESPONSIBILITY

Just as the writer has a responsibility to the site so does the site have a responsibility to the writer. A relationship cannot blossom if there is only one party giving and one party taking. I know this sounds like a Hallmark movie, but it's true.

- The blog admin should be active on social media–not just posting but conversing with readers and potential readers and supporting all writers on the site.
- Social media reach should be extensive and growing with real followers and friends.
- Site should promote each writer. There are some well-known sites who promote their featured bloggers or a small number of writers only. For these sites, promote your work mostly. There is no need to stay, chat and promote blogger #8015.
- Fresh content daily. If a site has new content only twice or three times a week, their reach is not growing. People get

bored quickly, so a site needs to have new material each day in order to attract readers.

While community sites do offer writers a lot of advantages, there are some downsides. It is up to you as a writer to figure out the best balance.

The Cons of a Community Blog

- The focus is on the whole and not each individual, but out of that "whole" some stars do emerge, and there is a chance you might not be one of them. Hey, we are all stars in one way or another just not everywhere. So don't get insulted; keep trying and you might reach the "star status."
- Your work will be on the top of the page for a short time. Each time someone posts, your work falls farther down the page.
- You are going to have to keep your ego in check. This is hard to do, but don't let it dissuade you from being the best writer you can be and enjoying the camaraderie on these sites.
- You will not like the humor of everyone on the site. Some humor will offend you. But each writer is trying to gain an audience, so unless their humor offends your moral sensibilities, offer support. That's all any writer wants on a community site.
- There are limited writing spots, which means you might get rejected as a writer initially. Keep applying and you will eventually get that spot if you give your best.

I don't know where to place this helpful tidbit so I'll throw it out here. Feel free to catch it and use it or let it fall. If a site doesn't pay you, it should not require you to post only original material. I understand if they request that you don't put up the same post on a competitor site on the same day or even the same week, but beyond that, no non-paying site should demand that your work be written only for them. So here's a secret. Sometimes it works and sometimes it doesn't, but it's a trick one of my magazine editors taught me a few years back, and it is helpful. Re-write your column or post for different outlets. **This only works for non-paying outlets.** For these non-paying sites, change the title so Google and other search engines find all the different titles. Honestly, if you use the same title over and over for several sites, search engines seem to get frustrated or ticked off and lose all the posts with that title. The conspiracy theorists out there believe they lose stuff on purpose.

So if you are not breaking a community site rule, change the post around, use a different angle, re-write the lead paragraph, switch up the humor helpers or dialogue—do whatever to make the post as original an essay as possible for wherever you post. Now, here's another caveat: Some sites frown upon this and declare it to be a big no-no. So always check with the site before you put too much effort in de-constructing and re-constructing your work.

If a site *pays* you, deliver an original post. Hand over that post with your first-born child if necessary. They are paying you dammit!

CHAPTER VII: Share And Care On Social Media

Many years ago, and it does feel like eons, I began to delve into what some people called the "dark world." No, I did not become a Satanist. I joined social media. In a way, it was a dark and mysterious place. I knew nothing about anything. The only experience I had with Facebook was watching my daughter turn on her account when she got to Penn State. Yes, it was a platform for college students only, and I never thought I would have to bother about meeting and talking with people through the vast internet.

Then, I started to write my humor online, and I realized that unless I learned to share my work, no one would find it. So I put on my big-girl boots and started to stomp through this scary world.

Twitter was my first stop. This platform seemed harmless enough. How much trouble can one get into when one can only use a maximum of 140 characters to communicate? Answer: You would be surprised.

It took me a while to realize there were so many imposters out there and to accept the fact that neither Edgar Allan Poe nor the Real Jesus had risen to chat with me. Despite my initial mistakes, I made the commitment to learn the platform. I read as much as I could, and I built my following slowly. A wise Twitter follower gave me advice that I still use: *Don't buy followers. Reach out and "meet" people.*

I started locally with Philadelphia people. I am a huge Phillies fan, and I could always find people to tweet with, especially during the games. Did these tweet friendships last? Yes, I've gone to games at Citizens Bank Park with Twitter friends. My writing sparked connections with other writers and artists as well. I met a wonderful guy from Great Britain, who through Twitter taught me how to bake fruit cake. In fact, on the day of my first effort into this culinary feat, he surrendered sleep so he could tweet with me as my cake baked in the oven. And how about this? I wouldn't be writing this book if it weren't for Twitter because on Twitter I met Carol Sabik-Jaffe, who is a board member of the Philadelphia Writers' Conference and who, after tweeting with me for some time, submitted my name to teach humor at the conference. I am in awe at how the world works sometimes.

My next challenge was Facebook. Somewhere between my daughter starting college and graduating from college, Facebook opened its doors to the old folk. I didn't embrace Facebook right away. I was a bit nervous about connecting with people from high school or grammar school, but I soon realized that this social platform would allow me to share my work in so many ways. I began to post short humor pieces to get people interested in my writing, and when HO came on the scene, I began to promote my writers there as well. I expanded my Facebook reach to include not only my personal page but a HumorOutcasts.com page and an HOPress-Shorehouse Book page. I also joined a few groups. To this day, I don't join hundreds of groups because I find that many of the same people are in the same groups, and I don't want to inundate Facebook friends and make them sick of my very presence.

I have a confession. I am not the best self-promoter. I love to promote other people, but I stumble when it comes to tooting my own horn—as little as that horn might be. But social media gave me the confidence to push out my work without feeling as if I am being narcissistic. Once I got over my shyness regarding Facebook, I started to look at other platforms such as LinkedIn, StumbleUpon,

YouTube, Tumblr, Pinterest and Instagram, and I found them equally fascinating.

I know that many people—especially writers—are on social media, but let's go through some of the most popular platforms and smart ways to use them anyway. As you probably know by now, this is not a textbook so my advice for social media stems from my experiences and how the various platforms helped me to expand my readership and the readership of my writers and authors. I won't give step-by-step tutorials on any social media as you can find the best directions for them on their websites or YouTube. If you are already a social media maven—that is excellent. But read along anyway in case there are some helpful hints you might find useful.

EMAIL

Before we get into the social media platforms, let's talk about the power of email and your writing. We all have friends and family, and we all email those friends and family. We send updates on our lives, photos of our kids, jokes that have circulated the internet, so why not your links to your writing? I know that people hate to get junk in their mail, but your writing is not junk. You are letting those who are nearest and dearest to you know that you do publish your work, and you are giving them a place to find that work.

I would not send ten emails a day to notify your friends about your writing. That would encourage your email recipients to kick your email address to the spam folder, and once you get in there, it's hard to dig out. A once-a-week email would work and be a welcome distraction from the many email offers for cheap drugs, penile enhancers and opportunities from Nigerian princes in need of "special agents" to distribute their wealth.

Grow your email list by asking people for their email addresses when you go to conferences and events. Always have your business card handy and be interested in what they do, and they will be interested in what you do.

When you do send out your notifications about your writing to your email list, be sure to add in the subject line that you are sending your latest work so they know not to delete it or send it to their SPAM file. With that quick email lesson out of the way, let's move on to the fun and fascinating world of social media.

FACEBOOK

I hate using the word "literally," but literally everyone and their mother is on Facebook. Okay, that is another exaggeration, but I have a license to exaggerate; I'm a humorist. Who knew that the middle-aged and even the ascending middle-aged (Politically Correct term for old) would embrace this social device as much as they do? But Facebook does offer a huge potential audience for writers, artists, entrepreneurs and charities. So the days of turning your nose up at this social media vehicle should be long gone.

Facebook is about so much more than posting a status. Facebook connects people who share family members, friendships, hobbies, professions and professional associations, volunteer work and so much more. And you can show off your pets. Ain't nothing better than that! So how do you expand your Facebook reach?

Friends: When I talk to Facebook virgins, the first concern they express is how to find friends. Finding friends is the easiest part of Facebook. Go to Facebook.com and register. Then, when your profile is active, search out people you know. Are your siblings, cousins, friends on Facebook? If so, send a friend request. Once you gain a few friends, you will be surprised how other family members, friends, colleagues and acquaintances ask to connect to you. As in all social situations—real and virtual—the key ingredient to building a friend base is to be nice and interested. This is my Facebook caveat, and this one is definitely for the Facebook newbies: NOT EVERYONE ON FACEBOOK IS A GOOD PERSON! There is a good chance that some man or woman will message you and tell you that he or she likes your smile or your eyes and that you look like a person he or she wants to get to know so you both can build a relationship together. Facebook is NOT

Match.com, Christian Mingle or even AshleyMadison. So if someone propositions you or proposes marriage, it's most likely not love at first sight. On Facebook, you can be as transparent as you want, but I do recommend some privacy barriers. When people ask you to be a friend, click on their profile to see if you share friends or if you can see any information about them. Sometimes, their privacy walls limit what you can see. The best advice I can give with this is CAUTION. If you friend someone and then realize he or she is on the FBI's Most Wanted List…or already in prison…hit the unfriend and block buttons. It's not hard to do.

There are certain unofficial "rules" you should follow on Facebook. I will admit that most of these rules are common sense, but, alas, much of our world does not run on common sense, so let's check out the rules.

WHAT TO DO ON FACEBOOK:

Like your friends' posts - You don't have to like every post of every friend, but make a point of going on Facebook and reading other people's posts. When you take an interest in their lives, they will take an interest in yours. To be honest, Facebook is a wonderful way to rekindle friendships and stay in touch with people you wish you had stayed connected to over the years. It is so much fun when I get a friend requests from women (girls school) I went to high school with more than 30 years ago. I love seeing their families and finding out about their lives. And for new friends, Facebook gives you a glimpse into their lives and a way to be a part of their lives.

Comment on posts - Again, there is no pressure to comment on every post, but it's nice to be happy for people or laugh with them or show compassion when their lives goes awry. If something really catches your attention, say so in a comment.

Be engaged (Sharing and Tagging) - Come on, who doesn't want to share a cute puppy post or photos of a new baby? Don't overuse these features but sometimes a post or photo is too good not to share with the world.

Hopefully, you joined Facebook as a way to share your writing work too. Let's not forget this important detail. Post the link to your blog posts so people find your work. It doesn't matter if you write on your own blog or a community blog or a few community blogs. Post that link—not all at once if it's the same post. If you give your Facebook friends too many links to choose from, they might be overwhelmed and go to none.

Posting a link to your writing on Facebook also brings in readers who do not get notifications about your work in their email. Seeing your link might inspire Facebook friends to subscribe to your blog so they can receive email notifications. Sharing your work on Facebook builds a fan base and as a writer isn't that what you want?

Join groups and share your work with those groups (carefully) - Why carefully? Many groups have rules about posting. Learn each group's rules before you throw your work on their feed. Some groups allow members to post only on certain days or in a certain way on the feed. Ask the group leader if you don't understand their rules. They won't yell at you. It's better to be sure so you don't alienate group founders or members.

Look for groups that are not in your normal comfort zone or maybe start a new group. Joining or creating a Facebook group that is not about writing or humor opens you up to the possibility of new readers and perhaps new material or new interests. It is only by expanding our horizons and relationships that we grow as writers. You might find that you win devoted fans who lie beyond the safety walls of your "normal" groups.

Don't be offended if some groups do not allow you to join. Some groups are private and are set up that way for a reason. The HumorOutcasts and HOPress Facebook group is open only to HO writers, HOPress-Shorehouse Books authors and a few close friends whom I rely upon to get out the word on the site or the publishing house. Why? Because when I send out email, no one reads it–yes, that's you, my writers and authors! But I love you all anyway. I'm going on the assumption my messages go into your spam folders and you forget to check those folders. Anyway, to remedy this communication challenge, I started a closed Facebook group. This way, my writers cannot "accidentally" delete me, and they get the necessary updates.

WHAT NOT TO DO ON FACEBOOK:

Sometimes I read posts on Facebook, and I want to jump through my computer monitor and shake the people who wrote those posts for giving out so much private information. I am probably paranoid about this, but I do worry about people who think they are safe on Facebook because they think only their friends can see what they post. Let's look at it this way: if computer hackers can steal your financial history from halfway around the world, someone can figure out how to see what you do, where you go and what you post even if he or she is not your Facebook friend. Your 14-year-old neighbor has probably read all about your life on Facebook even though you and he are not internet buddies anywhere. What can we learn from my paranoia?

Don't overshare. It's not necessary - In my almost thirty years as a humorist, I have read and worked with a lot of talented writers. To me, the hallmark of a great humorist is one where readers believe they know 100 percent about the life of that humorist, but in truth they only know about 10 percent.

What does that mean? Great humorists make their readers feel as if they are part of their everyday existence, but it's not the case. These humorists manage to share a portion of their lives, win the heart of their readers and still maintain their private life.

I think it's wonderful that Facebook allows us to share life and death moments with our friends because how would people across the country or on another continent know about births, weddings, deaths, etc.? However, I want people to be careful in their writing and in their posting. The more information you put out there, the less protection you have on a personal level. A few rules to live by:

Don't tear down another writer on Facebook. If you don't like someone's work, write a review and post that review on a suitable blog or site. Don't take personal shots when you probably share a lot of the same Facebook friends.

Your dislike of blog sites for which you write – You would assume that no writer would express this, but you would assume wrong. So let's touch on this briefly. If a site is helping you out, don't throw barbs at it and declare that you think you can run it better and more efficiently. That will not go over well with those who run the site, and they will find out.

Employment issues - Do not describe your boss using any unflattering or derogatory terms. He or she might not be your friend on Facebook, but chances are someone at work is, and they will happily rat you out. If you are one of those lucky, rare writers who have millions of dollars in the bank, then forget this warning because you won't care if you get fired over a controversial post.

Your medical history - Once you open that door, unscrupulous people can use that information to harm you in many ways, including attempts to steal your identity. Sure, you want to tell friends how that boob job went, and maybe you want to show them off too, but it might be best to do that in a closed group or perhaps a tasteful humor column that doesn't come with photos. I hate to say this, but you might lose the squeamish as friends if you give out too much information about blood and stitches.

Your travel schedule - I know people who post their airline schedules and the departure and return dates for their writers' conferences, vacations and business trips. If you do this, just make it easy for the burglar and post a banner that says, "Come rob me; I'm not home. I'll be back Thursday at 11 AM."

And most important:

Don't spend your entire day on Facebook or any other social media - Go out and live, meet people, write, have fun, go to the gym, eat a donut–whatever floats your boat. There are so many aspects to Facebook from tagging people and posting photos to playing games. Drop off social media for at least a few hours a day. Those cute puppies and funny jokes about wine, menopause and politicians will be there when you get back.

TWITTER

Twitter is a social platform for those who love to live in the brief present. You get 140 characters to deliver your message to thousands of people. Never in my wildest dreams did I ever think that I could master anything that would allow me only 140 characters to spit out my message in a coherent fashion. Was it worth my effort to learn? According to my Google analytics, yes. I tweet out my HO writers' posts each day at least once, and always readers from Twitter will click the link and visit the site to read that work. So I'm pretty sure Twitter would consider me a happy customer. I find Twitter to be an easy platform to use, but I know a lot of writers who get stymied with the 140-character rule because they don't want to take the time to compose the short posts.

A quick note: Twitter is experimenting with expanding the 140-character rule. Don't get too excited as I'm sure they won't allow 800-character tweets. Just in case the 140-character tweet remains the standard, still learn to be brief.

Learning to be brief can be a chore, and if you are trying to be brief and funny, you have a double challenge. When Twitter initially came on the scene, detractors seemed put off by Tweeps (people who use Twitter) who would send out tweets (the posts that are put out) about inane topics like buying shoes or the weather or the Kardashians. And, yes all of those things can be annoying.

However, I look at tweets as little glimpses into the lives of people I might not ever meet. And not only is that fun, but those tweets introduced me to so many talented writers whose books I have come to enjoy.

People devoted to Twitter use it for a variety of reasons, and these are some of the most popular reasons:

Celebrity stalking and entertainment - Okay, you might not truly be a stalker, but there is a reason why a celebrity has two million followers. Fans are checking out their appearance schedules, their love lives, their latest arrests…so much to know about your favorite stars.

Business promotion - Many businesses are on Twitter talking about new products or services or delivering coupons, specials, etc. Corporations also use Twitter to address customer service issues. There have been times when in-house customer service reps have treated me shabbily, so I took my beef to Twitter and within minutes my problem was resolved. No company wants negative tweets about their products or employees out there.

News - Broadcast and print media tweet out headlines, breaking news items or emergency information. It's a fast way to reach people and news outlets can get feedback from the Twitter world.

Books and entertainment promotion - I use Twitter daily to talk about my authors, writers and their work. Sometimes, no one sees a post, and other times you hit a target and your post is a success and retweeted or liked by hundreds of Twitter people.

I think a lot of people turn their backs on Twitter because they don't get how it works. Again, YouTube contains detailed lessons covering everything from building a profile to sharing tweets, but I will give you a quick and basic rundown of this social media platform. Here we go.

First go to Twitter.com and sign up. Pick a good password and be ready to switch it every six months. Why? Accounts get hacked, so having a few alternative passwords helps prevent this problem. In fact, follow this password advice for all your social media platforms. It's a smart idea to switch passwords at least twice a year.

Set up your profile and a twitter handle that reflects who you are. Notice that all Twitter handles or names begin with the @ sign. I have two accounts to cover both my site and my publishing company. My handles are @dtcav and @HOPress. Many Tweeps ask why I don't have an @Humoroutcasts handle. Well, as I explained in the social media introduction a few pages back, I was on Twitter long before HumorOutcasts.com came into existence, and I had a substantial following with @dtcav, so to change my Twitter name had two main disadvantages. First, @Humoroutcasts would have confused the followers of @dtcav who might have missed the name change, thus setting me up for a possible string of "unfollows." Second, @Humoroutcasts is a long Twitter name and would take up valuable character space in each tweet. A writer suggested I shorten it to @HO, but that might give Twitter people the wrong idea about me or even prompt the "Real Jesus" to unfollow me, and I wasn't sure what that meant for the afterlife, and finally, I would probably be screening porn messages from morning to night. So I decided to let @dtcav live as who has time to screen messages from Twitter people who can perform amazing things with body parts all day long?

Once you have your twitter handle, take the time to construct a good bio. I do not follow anyone without a bio. I can't tell if a "person" without a bio is human or a *spambot* who will try to access and harvest private information or infect my computers with viruses and worms. Another item that potential followers look for is a photo. If you do not share what you look like, the chances of people wanting to connect with you greatly decrease. I don't want to hear how you hate your photo. No one hates cameras more than I do. I am the queen of the not-photogenic, but I put up a picture and if nothing else, it amuses my Twitter followers.

I have a profile—now what? As is the case with Facebook, search for names of people you might know and ask to connect. Some Facebook friends will be on Twitter too, and you can follow them there. By the way, this happens with all the social media platforms. Your friends will overlap. That is kind of fun, and it will help build friendships. Twitter, like Facebook, also provides you with suggestions of people to follow. Once you get on Twitter, followers will find you. Others might disagree, but I am against buying Twitter followers or Facebook followers for that matter. I do not consider bought followers to be genuine followers. They make you look important, but do you want people to read your work and get to know you, or do you want to look important? Only you know what is best for you.

How do I build and organize my Tweeps? Twitter does allow you to create lists so you can organize your followers which makes it easy to track them down when you want to tweet out to them or find what they are posting. It's not a big deal to find your followers when you have a total of twenty, but if you have 10,000 followers, it becomes difficult. I keep about twenty lists that include HO writers, entrepreneurs and psychics and spiritual healers. (I'm a writer. Are you truly surprised by that last one?) Make lists for what interests you.

Hashtags: Social media newbies often ask about hashtags. What are they? Hashtags or the pound sign (#) are tags that can now be used on all social media not just Twitter. A hashtag makes one or more words searchable links. They are a great tool because hashtags do help you organize what you read and write. When you search on a hashtag, all posts about that topic will come up as well. I use the hashtags #humoroutcasts and #humor a great deal in my Twitter, Google, Tumblr and Instagram posts, and when people click on those hashtags, they will see my writers' work, which is wonderful.

HASHTAG EXAMPLE: Logic wins out? from @itsgoodtomock They should know better than to ask me these questions. http://humoroutcasts.com/2016/they-should-know-better-than-to-ask-me-these-questions/ ... #humoroutcasts #humor

In each tweet, I try to put in a funny or teaser introduction, but when one is limited to that 140-character count, it can prove to be impossible, especially if I want to insert a hashtag.

What should I post on Twitter? As a writer, you need to post LINKS TO ALL YOUR WORK OR BOOKS OR VIDEOS. Wherever you have your work, tweet out that site. Also if someone else is important in that tweet, refer to him or her in the tweet.

TWEET REFERENCE EXAMPLES:
Ready to #laugh out loud? from @Shiglyogly Bernadette Peters Hates Me: True Tales of a Delusional Man http://ow.ly/4ngOuh #humor

#Motherhood made not so perfect? from @DorothyRosby I DIDN'T KNOW YOU COULD MAKE BIRTHDAY CAKE FROM SCRATCH http://amzn.to/1r6RFN0 #humor

Twitter followers who are interested in humor, jokes, motherhood and even mommy bloggers will find these tweets.

I also work on my humor on Twitter. I will compose witty remarks or tweets to grab people's attention and hopefully this makes them want to go find out about me and then go to my site. When I am not in promotion mode, I tweet to friends about their families, recipes, sports interests and everyday lives. In other words, I stay engaged. I go to my home Twitter feed and I click on my lists so that I can see the tweets of people I follow. When I read interesting posts, I send a tweet to those who wrote them saying I enjoyed reading their posts or I click the heart icon under their tweets to express my like for them or the Retweet icon to share the tweets with my followers. And it snowballs from there. Twitter is a fun and easy platform – don't be afraid of it; embrace it.

What are the most important lessons of Twitter? Don't just tweet and never like or retweet anyone else's posts. Life is busy, and we all get busy. There are some weeks—and I am ashamed to admit this—I am a post and go person, but I always make up for it when I have the time. I apologize to the Twitter people whom I support and who support me the most. If you don't check in with Twitter once you join, you will miss out on followers, supporters and maybe some good comments about your work.

Be polite. If someone retweets or likes your tweet, say thank you. The internet is filled with angry people who because they are virtually anonymous scream and rant about everything. A little niceness goes a long way.

Be careful of the Twitter gurus who preach that the number of people who follow you should be greater than the number of people you follow. I don't buy this philosophy. As in life, make your twitter friends feel that you are interested in their tweets and posts and the followers will build, and they will look forward to your tweets. Do not try to manipulate the ratio of followers to those you are following. However, I do think it's a good idea to go through your Twitter friends every few months to figure out who you want in your Twitter world. There are free sites that keep track followers and those who have unfollowed you. You can google "Twitter followers" and a few pop up immediately. I use these sites just to make sure non-human followers have not invaded my Twitter feed.

LINKEDIN

I have a deep fondness for LinkedIn. As a humorist, I feel it is my responsibility to share funny stuff on this platform because I think the serious people who use LinkedIn need a good chuckle. LinkedIn is filled with marketing and financial articles and political correctness. It's fun to play with all those serious brains by posting humor. That being said, it is a professional crowd, so I don't post work with bad language or sexual overtones. I save those gems for other platforms where people are a little more loosey-goosey. Do my connections (friends in the LinkedIn world because the word "connections" has a far more professional tone to it) resent my sharing humor? Nope. HumorOutcasts.com receives a great deal of hits daily from LinkedIn. Everyone needs to laugh especially those who live in the high-stress world of business. The thing about LinkedIn is that some members frown on people trying to connect with anyone they don't know. The platform is about building business relationships, so they want to keep that professional vibe. Don't try and be everyone's best friend. LinkedIn does allow you to form groups as well and chat with experts, so it is a valuable platform. You can choose the free version or upgrade to a paid version that gives you more tools to identify possible connections or to pursue career opportunities.

INSTAGRAM

Instagram is a wonderful visual platform to share photos and videos. I go to Instagram when I want to show off a new book cover from HOPress-Shorehouse Books or a fun photo-centered post on HumorOutcasts.com. There is a great potential to engage people on Instagram and form connections as we live in such a visual world. My own granddog, Theo, known on Instagram as THEO_THEGSD, has more than 20,000 followers. If a German shepherd puppy can post on Instagram without the advantage of opposable thumbs to click on the app, think what you can do. (For the sake of legal stuff and accuracy, I'm pretty sure my daughter and son-in-law do the Instagram postings for Theo, but he does tell them what to say.) Instagram allows users to partner with other followers, and this in turn sets up many sharing possibilities. It is a great tool for promotion.

YOUTUBE

What did we do before instructional videos on YouTube? I have learned everything from tying a scarf to Pilates exercises to relighting the pilot light on my gas fireplace from YouTube. YouTube is the teacher of all teachers, and let's not forget, this platform has launched quite a few celebrity careers. Some of our writers have ventured into the video world, and when they post humorous videos and short films on YouTube, we share the links on Humoroutcasts.com. I also use YouTube to post our HOPress-Shorehouse Books trailers and television interviews that our writers and authors do. And as I said at least twice now, YouTube has video instructions for learning all the social media platforms.

GOOGLE +

I have become fans of writers whom I never would have found had it not been for Google +. I joined several communities on this platform, and I enjoy commenting, chatting and sharing on Google +. It's my first stop when I want to see what my favorite authors and bloggers are up to. It is an easy-to-use platform and still has so much growth ahead of it. I highly recommend this social media outlet.

PINTEREST

When Pinterest first surfaced, it intimidated me. I thought I had to know how to bake. There were so many photos of decadent desserts and culinary masterpieces that I assumed you had to know how to create these things and not just eat them. Then, I noticed Pinners (Pinterest people) creating new boards about cute dogs, home design, gardening, humor etc., and I was hooked. In Pinterest, Pinners create virtual bulletin boards and pin photos and articles to these boards and share them with other Pinners. When other Pinners see these photos and boards, they, in turn, can like and share and pin them to their own boards, and this is how the Pinterest world works. It is an ingenious platform for sharing, and it is visually attractive as well. To this day, I think the person who designed Pinterest should win a Nobel Prize in something. Is there a Nobel Prize for social media? There should be, and the person behind Pinterest should win it hands down.

Once my obsession with Pinterest had taken root, I created my own boards. Now, I have an HO (HumorOutcasts.com) board, A Little Comic Relief board, an HOPress-Shorehouse Books board and several others. On most of my boards I can promote my writers and authors, and this ability has helped me get their names out there. I promise that if you sign on to Pinterest, you will never regret it. When my daughter was engaged and we were planning her wedding, we created a private board, and we shared ideas between the two of us on that board. Enough said on Pinterest; I am obviously a big fan.

STUMBLEUPON

Stumbleupon.com takes some work to learn and it does require mastering a fair number of technical issues, but I rely on this site. They welcome fresh content daily on all topics, and not only do I share my writers' work here, but I learn so much from other Stumblers (the Stumbleupon network). There are wonderful writers, teachers, artists, health experts…you name it, they have articles on it. When you find a post or article you like, you can share it, like it and stumble it, which puts it out to all the other Stumblers on the platform. Humoroutcasts.com receives hundreds of visitors a day from Stumbleupon. It might not be the most "user-friendly" platform, but if you like to read and look at photos (so many talented artists and photographers post their work here), check out StumbleUpon.com

TUMBLR and REDDIT

I save these two social media sites for my edgier and younger writers as the younger-than-boomer age group seems to be the demographic for these sites. When I look at HO's site analytics, we do get quite the number of 18-to-25-year-old readers, and I would bet that most of these readers come from these platforms. So it does not matter that I am personally not in this demographic; a good number of my readers are, so I will share my writers' work on both of these sites.

While I talked about the more well-known platforms, there are hundreds more that are directed at specific groups. Unfortunately, I cannot go into all of them here. Just when you think you have seen the newest social media craze, another one pops up. That is the world we live in today. No one can learn all of them. There are only twenty-four hours in a day, so pick the ones you feel most comfortable using and go from there, and don't feel guilty for not visiting each platform daily. Breathe, relax and visit when you can. Remember, social media is about being social and enjoying the "company" of those who share that platform.

Managing social media: If you find that you are time-challenged and cannot log on to each platform daily, there is help for you. There are social media scheduling platforms such as Hootsuite—there are others out there too—that allow you to see all your social media feeds on one page and give you the opportunity to schedule and share posts to the various platforms or analyze the effect a post had on those platforms. Some of these social media management sites have a free version and an upgraded pay version that gives you more detailed information so you can choose what fits your needs best.

Another important fact of social media to know is that you can advertise on all of them. Yes, it costs you money, but if you want to compose an ad for your blog, book, video or whatever, you can do so. Advertising on social media is not expensive compared to other forms of advertising, and it allows you to target the audience you want to reach.

PART III: HOW CAN I GET MY BOOK PUBLISHED?

Oh, how the world of publishing has changed! Traditional publishers still hold clout, but they are not the only game in town. A variety of publishing platforms give authors a chance at their dream. What are your options as an author?

CHAPTER VIII: Can I Still be a Paperback Writer?

I love the song "Paperback Writer" by the Beatles. I feel the frustration and urgency of the "writer" as he sings his query letter to any publisher who will listen. What has changed since that song was released in the 1960s? That fictional writer had a better chance of finding a traditional publisher than most writers do today. If you write in the humor genre, you probably have a better chance of being struck down by lightning twice and eaten by a shark in the same day than you do signing a traditional publishing contract. Oh, the negativity—I know, but, alas, it's true.

In the last decade, the publishing industry has gone through upheaval after upheaval. Is this such a bad thing? In some ways, yes and in some ways, no. I watch *Murder, She Wrote* reruns on TV, and it's sad that the old-style of publisher who caters to writers and pays their expenses to send them on exciting book tours is no more. Isn't that the romantic image we all held as writers? Oh, there are a few authors who still get the "celebrity" treatment, but chances are they were celebrities before they were authors or bestselling writers before the tumultuous changes in the publishing industry occurred, so this star treatment is nothing new for their lives. Still, many writers clamor for the chance at a traditional publishing contract, and I can understand that desire, and I will always support it.

In this section, I don't want to influence your opinion about any type of publishing. I want you to know your options when it comes to getting your book published. Whatever way you get published, I say CONGRATULATIONS! You worked hard for that book, and I will celebrate that accomplishment.

As I said before, this is not a textbook, so I am not going to throw facts and figures at you about any type of publishing. I want to share with you my experiences and what led me to the HOPress-Shorehouse Book business model. No publishing model is right for everyone. If I could, I would wave a magic wand and give all writers the publishing contract of their dreams.

Why I got into the publishing business:

I touched upon my reasons for becoming a publisher in the introduction of the book. I did not plan on being a publisher. My plan was to help humor writers find an audience. As writers gained more confidence and developed their fan bases, some wanted to fulfill their dreams of being authors. Unfortunately, there were no traditional publishing contracts to be had for humorists. Literary agents laughed humorists out of their offices. Some wouldn't return phone calls. It was during this frustrating time that three separate writers emailed me within a week of each other to see if I could somehow publish their books.

After doing quite a bit of research, I realized that I could form an imprint publishing house and get my writers' work published. I named it HumorOutcasts Press because HumorOutcasts.com was doing so well and gaining readers daily. I figured that had to help my authors. I truly thought I would be helping only humorists. However, within six months, writers of other genres asked for my publishing help, and I hesitated because I felt that the name HumorOutcasts Press did not fit well for other genres. The writers insisted I look at their work, so I created the Shorehouse Books imprint to go along with HumorOutcasts Press, so now writers can go to HOPress-ShorehouseBooks.com and get information for all genres. Once I added the second imprint, the publishing company took off. I still cannot take on all authors, but what I learned is that there is so many talents out there who deserve to have their books published, and I want to make that happen.

For a year and a half, we experimented with several publishing models that ranged from no payments upfront to our current model which requires either a one-time upfront payment or a deposit with a scheduled payment plan. In my opinion, HOPress-Shorehouse Books is a Partner Publisher. Some people use the term subsidy publisher and others use boutique publisher, but boutique publishers used to refer to publishers that handled certain niches. I guess with everything in the publishing world, that definition has grown to include subsidy or partner publishing, but I'm still not sure if HOPress fits that mold. For HumorOutcasts Press-Shorehouse Books, I like the term *Partner Publisher*—somewhere between traditional and vanity publishing with vanity publishing requiring a much larger investment from the author. Vanity publishing does provide some perks such as hardcover books, and some established vanity publishers do provide a gateway to a second-edition traditional publishing contract. For HOPress-Shorehouse Books, our motto is *Independent Publishing with a Traditional Flair*. We are truly a mix, but it does work for us and our authors.

There are still the publishing snobs out there who think that to go the subsidy, partner or vanity press route is to admit that as an author, one has no talent. I truly dislike this attitude. To me, it is a fear-fear attitude as opposed to a win-win attitude. These critics are afraid that someone using the non-traditional paradigm will create a bestseller and make the work of traditionally published authors less important. Excuse me while I channel my Latin teacher, Sister Felician, who used to say, "Building yourself up by knocking others down is just plain bad." And she used to say it in Latin. Damn, I loved that woman. Okay, back to the publishing point. The world changes, and you either adapt or become extinct.

Let's be honest. Is there any perfect publishing model? No. But it is damn hard to sell books no matter what method of publishing a writer uses, so any model that helps achieve that goal has its benefits. It takes commitment to be an author. It is a difficult path, but a worthwhile one. I wish I could offer more options for authors to make their publishing journey a bit easier, but that's not the writing world in the present day. Since we began publishing in late 2012, we have published more than 40 titles, and I have authors-to-be submitting work on a weekly basis. In 2016, we added a business imprint, Corner Office Books, for entrepreneurs and business leaders who realize they need a book for speaking engagements or to cement their status as experts in their field. For HOPress-Shorehouse Books, the learning curve has been a steep one but so much fun. And with each release, our name gets more attention and so do our authors, and I guess that's what our goal was all along.

Do we hold a monopoly on this model? Absolutely not, and I like that fact. I admire other companies that have formed subsidy or partner publishing houses especially the oh-so-proper big publishers who now see the value in this type of publishing. I believe that as our publishing model gains more ground, writers stand a better chance of finding a publishing company that fits their needs. I think brick-and-mortar booksellers, who have already started to thaw their attitude about non-traditional publishers, will continue to open their doors to these authors without restrictions.

What it comes down to is this: Publishing today makes me scream with delight. It is so exciting. I feel as if we are all witnessing the birth of a new world—one where authors and publishers have equal stake in the process, and that is wonderful.

It's important that authors understand the four main publishing models that exist today so that they can pursue the best option for their writing needs.

TRADITIONAL PUBLISHING

When a writer dreams of a traditional publishing contract, that dream begins with a literary agent who uses his or her keen negotiating skills to secure a big-name publisher for a talented author. There is no cooler fantasy for writers than getting an email or phone call from a literary agent in New York or Los Angeles who says, "I am going to represent you and get you a five-figure advance."

Alas, this fantasy rarely occurs. You might get an agent and/or a contract, but the five-figure advance is tough to get if you are not already famous. But let's say the Universe heard your request and sends you a traditional publishing contract. It's good to know the advantages and disadvantages of traditional publishing before you sign on the dotted line.

Advantages of Traditional Publishing:

- You have name recognition behind your book.
- If you are a well-known celebrity, athlete or a recent headline in the news, you stand a good shot of getting that book tour we all dream about.
- You have an in-house editor to review your book and make changes and an in-house cover designer.
- Your traditional publisher might print hardcover copies of your work.
- You have the chain bookstores and independent bookstores willing to carry your book.
- You don't pay the costs of returned books from bookstores. That cost is on your publisher.
- You will have some marketing support (at least for the first month of a book's release).
- You pay no upfront costs.

Disadvantages of Traditional Publishing:

- You will be giving your publisher between 75 and 90 percent of your royalties for paperbacks, and if they do eBooks, they will receive a similar royalty structure. Your royalty percentage could increase or decrease as more books sell. It depends on the contract and your clout as an author.
- Your in-house editor might have control over the content of your book. You might not be consulted on changes or edits.
- You might not have a say in your cover design.
- Although they should provide some marketing support, the majority of marketing and promotion will fall in your lap.
- Your book cannot be topical as traditional publishers can take up to three years to release a book. If they sign other books they consider more topical or marketable, they can push your book release back.
- You might have to take a backseat to celebrity authors or bestselling authors already on their client list.
- You can't get in the door of a traditional publisher without a literary agent, and they are as difficult to contract as publishers.

SUBSIDY OR PARTNER PUBLISHING

Whatever you want to call this business model, know you will have to make an initial investment in your book. Some companies provide an a la carte menu in an attempt to work with any budget, so it's important that you understand the services you need and compare the prices for these services and what they include. They vary widely from publisher to publisher, so take your time and talk to different companies.

Advantages of Subsidy or Partner Publishing:

- You don't need an agent and you will have a REAL publisher.
- You don't have to know anything about publishing or how to get a book into print.
- You get a higher royalty percentage than you do with traditional publishers. AND you should get regular royalty statements and payments.
- You maintain control of your book project.
- Any changes or edits must meet with your approval and/or you can choose to contract your own editor.
- There is a short release window between submission of final manuscript and release or you can select your release date.
- Partner publishers SHOULD handle everything from the purchase of ISBNs to formatting the book to the release of the book and marketing if you want that service.
- You can choose services such as cover design and editing and are not forced to use any services you don't need. Partner publishers should offer some basic promotion in their initial package cost. They have to do some promotion to sell books so they make a profit as well.

- If you pay for promotion and marketing, publishers should write press releases, set up author pages for you on their website, send out review requests, send out interview requests, compose media lists and follow up with those lists and send out a number of review copies too.
- Many partner and subsidy publishers use Print-on-Demand or POD publishing platforms, which means authors should not be required to inventory books.
- Well-respected partner publishers who use POD platforms do use Ingram to distribute their books, and therefore they are available for purchase for all bookstores.
- Well-respected partner publishers will offer both paperback and eBook formats.
- Books get great online exposure through online retailer sites.
- Many established writers are abandoning traditional publishing for partner publishing because of the freedom they have with the production of their books and the royalty structure.

Disadvantages of Subsidy and Partner Publishers:

- You will have to pay upfront costs. Costs vary from publisher to publisher and services offered.
- You do not have an editorial team at your disposal. In other words, if you pay for editing, it is one editor. If you choose to hire your own editor, you will be responsible for delivering a ready-to-go manuscript to your publisher.
- Even if you sign on for marketing and promotion, you will have to be ready to self-promote. That's why it is called partner publishing. This model is about teamwork.

- You will have to embrace social media to get the word out.
- If you choose not to pay for promotion, you will have to write your own press releases, send out pitches to set up interviews and reviews or risk not selling any books.
- Bookstores might be hesitant about working with subsidy or partner publishers because POD sites do not pay bookstores for returned books. If your publisher does get your book in a brick-and-mortar bookstore, you might have to pay for warehousing fees for books that do not sell or for return fees. Some larger subsidy publishers do offer the option of adding protection against this returned book cost for an additional fee in their publishing package for a certain period of time following the release of a book.

VANITY PUBLISHING:

Vanity publishing has been around almost as long as traditional publishing. Some industry experts consider subsidy and vanity publishing to be the same thing, but I disagree. Vanity publishing requires a much larger investment and does not usually use a POD platform for its books. Some authors pay in excess of $10,000 for a Vanity publishing contract. However, the products are high-quality and there is still a publisher name on the copyright page.

Advantages of Vanity Publishing:

- More options for book production such as color illustrations, book size and paper weight
- Most vanity publishers do offer hardcover books, so for writers penning gift books, this might be the best platform available.
- Well-known vanity publishers are watched by traditional publishers and might attract traditional publishers to a writer's work.
- Authors do have a say in cover design and editing.
- The turn-around from submission to release is shorter than that of traditional publishing.
- Bookstores will carry books released by vanity publishers but depending upon the publisher, the warehousing costs might still be on the author.

Disadvantages of Vanity Publishing:

- It's still hard to overcome the stigma of vanity publishing.
- The costs usually run more than $10,000 which is a much greater investment than what is needed for subsidy or partner publishing.

- Vanity publishers that do not utilize POD might require authors to inventory a large number of books, which increases the authors' investment for publication.
- Not all vanity publishers offer uniform services, so writers have to investigate carefully as they would with subsidy and partner publishers.

SELF-PUBLISHING:

Fed up with the world of publishing, some writers have decided to go it alone. I admire these writers because I think they show great courage. Those who are tech savvy, should probably not have a problem with the self-publishing process itself but if you are a person who can't change the ink in your printer, think twice and then think one more time about going the self-publishing route. Self-publishing will require research and the ability to format your book. POD companies such as Amazon do offer assistance for self-publishers, but you have to pay for that assistance. So before you make the commitment to self-publishing, figure out your costs and time commitment. If you are confident you can handle both, go for it!

Advantages of Self-Publishing

- If you are comfortable with technology, it will be the most economical way to produce a book.
- You share no royalties with anyone except the POD company who publishes your work.
- You have TOTAL control over every aspect of the book.
- You can bring in consultants and experts as you need them.
- With lower upfront costs, you can spend more money on marketing and promotion, which you WILL need to spend.

Disadvantages of Self-Publishing:

- The production of the book is only the first step to a successful book launch. If you are an author/book publishing novice, you will learn hard lessons as you have no expertise in the book publishing world.
- You have to take on the "General Contractor" role and hire your cover artist, editor, proofreader and promotion

specialist, and those costs might surprise you. You also have to coordinate deadlines with these people and set up virtual or real meetings too. And guess what? Your boss might not understand your taking time out for all your book stuff...go figure.

- You will discover how time consuming promotion will be. Don't get discouraged. You will build confidence as a promoter. And if you have a nice family, they will buy books and help you promote too—well, except your teenage kids. They will deny you wrote anything.

- You will have to counter the negative image that many still possess for a self-published author. (Some media outlets will not talk to self-published authors.) For the record, this negative image is ridiculous. I have read more talented self-published authors than traditionally published ones in the last few years, so don't let anyone rock your confidence.

Some Ponderings about Publishing

When I speak about publishing, writers ask so many questions, but the questions that pop up all the time are those about my goals as a writer and experiences as a writer and publisher. I want to share these questions with you.

If a traditional publisher offered to publish one of my books would I turn them down?

I would have to think about it. I would never say no without weighing the pros and cons. Traditional publishers have published my work in the past, and I do get the appeal. But now as a partner publisher, I would probably pass unless, of course, they offer me the **Murder, She Wrote** publishing package complete with the whirlwind book tour with accommodations at the most expensive hotels throughout the world that come with pre-paid spa packages. Hey, I'm committed to my authors, but I'm not stupid. I know what a good massage is worth.

What are my biggest frustrations with publishing today?

1) The closed-door policy of traditional publishers and literary agents.
2) The negative attitude that both writers and non-writers still possess about non-traditional methods of publishing.
3) The idea that the publisher is solely responsible for book promotion.
4) The false notion that subsidy/partner publishers and self-published authors put out low-quality books and covers.

Sometimes people are caught in a time warp or they possess biases that are no longer true. In fact, today's vanity, partner and self-published books are just as high-quality as those released by traditional publishers.

CHAPTER IX: Go Forth and Spread Laughter!

I know that because you read this short book, you won't be an expert humor writer. It's taken me thirty years to achieve my level of expertise, and I'm still learning. I still get nervous about posting a piece or essay. I truly want you to understand that the most talented writers have essays or posts that fall flat. It's okay if that happens. Humor is so subjective, and you have to realize that not everyone is going to like your work. The earlier you realize that, the funnier you will become because you will remove the self-imposed weight of comic genius from your shoulders.

One final note: If you cannot tell, I am serious about humor. There is no greater gift than giving people the opportunity to let go of all their stress to laugh. If we could all learn to do this more often, the world would be a much kinder place. Never let anyone try to tell you that humor is superfluous or unimportant fluff. When you do run across those people—and you will—pity them because they have lost the meaning of what it means to be human, or better yet, tell them a joke unless of course, they look like they might hurt you. Then, just walk away.

In closing, thank you for allowing me to share my experiences and knowledge with you. Not all of you will agree with what I teach, but that's okay. Feel free to create your own spin and try out your own ideas. If you want feedback on your writing exercises or blog posts or writing goals, contact me:

Donna@Humoroutcasts.com or
Donna@HOPress-ShorehouseBooks.com

You can still try Betsy too. Maybe a Ouija board would be the most direct path for her though. Nah! I'm kidding. She still has an email address: Betsy@Humoroutcasts.com. One of us will get back to you.

Humor Inspiration: Bill Y Ledden

Humor writing is about writing humor. It's about deep, passionate hatred. When you hate Bon Jovi more than all the films of Will Smith and his family of talentless actors, you'll never be without material. Humor writing is observing the minute and blowing it so much out of proportion that it leaves the reader in no doubt that you're extracting the wee wee. Humor writing is taking the absurd, putting it through a creative process and ending up with something that makes ridiculous nonsense. Humor writing is about grabbing the rules and bending them so much that their only career choice is Artistic Gymnastics. There are tried and tested ways of making someone laugh but instead of learning these, dip your feet so far in the water that it covers your head and make it up as you go along. You'll find your own creative process and an identity that will give you a voice as distinct as Pavarotti singing John Lennon's "Imagine" without lyrics.

Bill Y Ledden is a mysterious Irish humorist who visits HumorOutcasts.com daily. His talents for Photoshop, captions and mocking have made his work go viral more times than the editors of HumorOutcasts.com can count. Some say Bill Y uses his humor to address his contempt for Bon Jovi and some Hollywood actors. This might be true, but whatever his goal, he keeps readers laughing on a daily basis while maintaining his ultra-secret identity.

Humor Inspiration: Bill Spencer

Like sex, humor is best when other people are involved. (For the graphic, uncensored working out of the lewd, lascivious, dirty details of this sex analogy, see the fourth paragraph.)

When I was a younger man, a month ago, some people told me creating humor was ridiculously easy, and I believed them, but now that I'm older I realize they were absolutely right. Sometimes I get lucky and read something I myself think is funny—like the fact that 5 of the 100 women in a Maxim survey said "It's so hot when a man . . . cooks"--and I'm able to use that as a springboard to make fun of myself, in this case my lack of hotness. But usually I focus on something that bothers me, such as student reviews calling me a "COMPLETE jerk" or "overall the DEVIL" or the time my five-year-old stepson jumped up and down on my shadow, right in the crotch-al area.

So the biggest source of inspiration for my humor writing is myself—my own quirks, failings, and failures. The humor comes when I'm able to see myself through others' eyes: my bungling as a Scout "leader," my storied trumpet-playing "career," or how my wife might see my incessant punning as less hilarious than I do. I love to play. I'm a kid who refused to grow up. It seems to me that to be a humorist it's important to play with language, to play with others, and, above all, it's important to play with yourself.

Bill Spencer's humor writing has been published by Funny Times, Narrative magazine, Reader's Digest, The Inconsequential, Clever magazine, Defenestration, HumorOutcasts.com, The Short Humour Site, Hobo Pancakes, and Nuthouse. He has also published scholarly articles on the novels of Cormac McCarthy. He lives in a cabin in the mountains of North Carolina with his wife, artist-poet Carolyn Elkins.

Humor Inspiration: Heidi Clements

For me, humor can be found in any situation, from a night with friends to a morning at the supermarket. From walking my dog to getting my nails done – when something ridiculous happens within the mundane – it never fails to make me laugh. What inspires me to write about those humorous situations is some bizarre desire to share my embarrassment with others. Most people don't feel comfortable revealing those red-faced moments in life but I seem to revel in it. Maybe if I write about the things everyone has gone through but is too afraid to say – it will help some others find the laughter in their own embarrassment. I took a soak in a hot spring this weekend that I'm quite certain was filled with human waste. That makes me laugh.

Heidi Clements is an Executive Producer and Writer on the Freeform show Baby Daddy. She writes a blog called "Welcome To Heidi" and can be found wasting her time on Instagram, Snapchat, and Facebook under the same name. She hopes to one day rule the world or at least perfect a pineapple upside down cake.

Humor Inspiration: Cathy Sikorski

Humor writing may be the most disrespected genre in the literary world. Many would say it does not even rise to a place where it deserves the name "literary." Nevertheless, this is where I have chosen to hang my writer's hat because it is my view of the world. I find nothing less inspiring, calming or easing of tension than using humor. Who wouldn't want to live in a laughing world as long as possible every single day?

Some might look at my journey so far and say it has been daunting and incredible. Incredible by its very definition which means not to be believed. But to be given the job, even tangentially, as a caregiver for seven different family members and friends over the past 25 years has been a grace underscored by volumes of humor.

I would say humor inspires my writing, but the attitude that it's all truly very funny at some point, either in the moment or looking back, is the gift I've been given. As a caregiver, I have encountered much frustration, anger, and disappointment. As a lawyer, it's pretty much the same. As a humorist, it is a constant rainbow of material and an opportunity to look at life in a much different way.

I love humor writing. I love sarcasm, ranting, puns and insults to myself—I love it all. I will likely stay a humor writer throughout my career as it gives me great joy, great internal and external power, and apparently is a very healthy way to live and look at life.

Cathy Sikorski is the author of Showering with Nana: Confessions of a Serial Killer Caregiver. She has been a significant caregiver for the last 25 years for seven different family members and friends. A published humorist, Sikorski is also a practicing attorney who limits her practice to Elder Law issues. Her combined legal and humor expertise has made her a sought after speaker and radio guest where she tackles the Comedy of Caregiving and the legal issues that affect those who will one day be or need a caregiver (which is everyone). Sikorski has participated in memoir writing classes for two years at the prestigious Fine Arts Work Center in Provincetown, Massachusetts. She has also participated in the Philadelphia Writer's Conference where she won a Humor Prize in 2014. Sikorski blogs for The Huffington Post and is a contributing author for HumorOutcasts.com

Humor Inspiration: Roz Warren

There's comedy all around you, if you pay attention. For instance? One day I arrived at the library where I work to find this sign posted on the front door: "The library's computers are not working today, which means that you will not be able to check out material unless you have your library card. We're very sorry for the incontinence."

Spell check strikes again!

I broke up. But I also thought: I can use this. And I did, in a humor piece about library work. Humor writing can be about coming up with, then developing, a good premise. But a lot of it is just noticing (and enjoying) The Funny, and then passing it along.

Roz Warren, "the world's funniest librarian," writes for The New York Times, The Funny Times, The Christian Science Monitor, The Jewish Forward, The Huffington Post and HumorOutcasts.com. And she's been featured on the Today Show. (Twice!) Roz's latest book, Our Bodies, Our Shelves: A Collection of Library Humor, has earned rave reviews from fans and empathetic librarians throughout the world. She is also the editor of the ground-breaking Women's Glib humor collections, including titles like The Best Contemporary Women's Humor, Men Are From Detroit, Women Are From Paris and When Cats Talk Back. Check out her website at www.rosalindWarren.com

Humor Inspiration: Mary Farr

I might have been ten years old when my father, an upstanding circuit court judge, handed me a gift-wrapped copy of Damon Runyon's *Guys and Dolls*. While this might have seemed like an odd choice of reading material for a ten-year-old girl, it suited me well. I had already fallen in love with the feckless, adorable gambler Nathan Detroit. Frankly, Runyon's outrageously silly characters made such an impression on me that Nicely Johnson and Harry the Horse appeared in my recent book *Never Say Neigh* (no surprise, co-written with my own horse).

In short, my father The Judge understood the meaning of funny and shared his gift with our extended family early and often. A quintessential storyteller, he paid attention to details that others missed. For example, when my grandparents' elderly Norwegian housekeeper, Clara Christianson, explained how her husband died, nobody but The Judge heard her say the man died of "Applestrokesy." This irregular version of the medical condition apoplexy soon found its way into the Farr humor lexicon.

The humor business spread like poison ivy through the family. Someone was always itching to regale the rest of us with a droll piece of trivia. Irreverent tales about deer hunting camp, Prohibition, weasels diving into occupied sleeping bags, Lena Tarbox slugging the district attorney with her purse in the courtroom, Artie Sullivan piloting his new Cadillac into Elk Creek—these tales and more punctuated our dinner conversation. My mother just rolled her eyes.

Somehow, I concluded at about age eleven that I must be Damon Runyon's protégé. Hence, I started writing humor, or at least what seemed funny to me. My first book, *I Think My Brother Likes Me,* failed due to what the editor called inappropriate treatment of our Labrador retriever Sam. Actually, we loved Sam, and all we did was hide him in the car trunk for a hasty ride to school for Show and Tell. It was awhile before I submitted another manuscript to a humorless editor.

So here it is fifty years later, and nothing has changed. My brother has picked up where The Judge left off. I continue to blog for a horse named Noah, a bit of a stretch even in the humor world. The best part is we all learned to laugh out loud at ourselves and at our observations of our world around us. Maybe that was the real humor lesson The Judge was angling for.

Mary Farr, a retired health care executive and pediatric hospital chaplain, has devoted thirty years to exploring the worlds of hope, healing and humor. Today, she has merged these life essentials into her newest book, The Promise in Plan B, What We Bring to the Next Chapter in Our Lives. Mary's capacity to infuse audiences with joy and confidence inspires compassion and a rich understanding of happiness. Mary is also the author of the award-winning Never Say Neigh: An Adventure in Fun, Funny and the Power of Yes which was written through the eyes of her horse Noah Vail.

Humor Inspiration: Deb Martin-Webster

I was a very inquisitive kid, always wanting to know how things worked. My key talent was breaking things while trying to figure out how they worked. This talent got me into lots of trouble, causing my mom and dad major headaches and costly repair bills. After numerous time-outs to reflect on my dastardly deeds, I had an epiphany. I discovered that I could get out of trouble if I made my parents laugh. So I began making fun of the way our next-door neighbor sneezed, the weird way my aunts and uncles chewed, imitating my nerdy school teachers – the list goes on.

As I matured, if you can call a permanent case of arrested development maturing, I started writing humorous anecdotes about everyday life, places I've visited and situations that seem to be normal but are completely insane if you think about them—for instance, people getting butt implants and other people trying to get rid of their big butts. Why don't they just organize a swap meet? But I digress. As a writer I make it a point to add my unique sense of humor to my novels, infusing a bit of it in the characters I create. And, when all else fails, I fall back on the "I've got your nose!" trick – it never gets old!

After a successful career in Art Administration at Temple University/Tyler School of Art, Deb has taken on a new challenging career as an aspiring writer.

Author of the short story "A Hot Dog Stand in the Himalayas," Deb has written two western romances: Love, Montana and Always, Montana. Forever, Montana is now in the works.

Deb is an original HOer as well. You can check out her popular series "Friday Humor Devotional," prayer with an attitude.

Humor Inspiration: Dorothy Rosby

A few years back, I was stopped for speeding. I don't mean to imply that that's only happened to me once. But this particular time was unusual in that instead of sitting and fuming while the officer went back to his car to write my ticket and check my outstanding warrants (and no, I didn't have any), I pulled out a notebook and started making notes for a column on speeding tickets. I tell you this because it explains where my inspiration comes from, which is every stupid thing that happens to me, but mostly the ones that weren't very funny while they were happening.

If I can have only one talent, and apparently that's all I get, I can't think of one I'd rather have than finding humor where at first glance, there doesn't seem to be any. And in case you're wondering, since that first column on speeding tickets, I've been "inspired" to write two more.

Dorothy Rosby is an author and syndicated humor columnist whose work appears in publications in eleven Western and Midwestern states. Her column has been recognized by the South Dakota Newspaper Association, the South Dakota Federation of Press Women, and the National Federation of Press Women. Her latest release is I Didn't Know You Could Make Birthday Cake From Scratch: Parenting Blunders from Cradle to Empty Nest. She is also the author of the humor book I Used to Think I Was Not That Bad and Then I Got to Know Me Better.

Humor Inspiration: Keith Stewart

I find inspiration for writing humor by being open to the possibilities each day presents to me. Most of the pieces I write involve my getting into some sort of embarrassing or uncomfortable situation. Like most people, I am mortified or humiliated or just downright ashamed as the actual event is happening. But afterwards, when I am safely back in my comfort zone and away from the actual scene, I start to think about what happened to cause me to feel that way.

At this point, I have a choice. I can continue to feel bad about the public embarrassment I have inflicted on myself, recoil to the bed, hide under the covers, and swear never to return to that particular place again, or I can examine the situation as a third party would have seen it. If I can imagine myself as an innocent bystander watching what happened, more often than not, I begin laughing. Once the laughter hits, my decision is made. I have to write about it.

For instance, just last week I had an appointment with a doctor. During the visit, it was determined I needed a shot. I stripped down to my skivvies for the nurse, and she injected me with medicine. As I undressed for bed later that night, I realized I had worn my underwear backwards all day, including the ten minutes or so I was standing around in nothing but shorts at the doctor's office in front of several people. I was initially horrified at myself. I decided I would have to find a new doctor because that one would surely think I was mentally unstable. But as I thought more about it, I imagined what the reaction of the nurse must have been when she saw me standing there. I began to get tickled; then I laughed. At that moment, inspiration struck for a great humor piece on going to the doctor.

While not everyone may wear his or her underwear backwards in public, everyone does experience embarrassing moments. It's a universal fact that we all make fools of ourselves at some point. By writing about mine, I think it helps people know they aren't alone in these crazy mishaps, and whatever it is that they feel terrible about may not be so bad after all.

Readers of my book or blog are constantly telling me hilariously embarrassing stories that happened to them. They feel safe telling me what happened because they know I can relate to their struggle to save face in public. Having that connection with people further inspires me to keep on looking for humor in everything that happens to me. I know that humor is there. Even if it's hard to find at first glance, it's waiting to be found.

Keith Stewart is the author of Bernadette Peters Hates Me – True Tales of a Delusional Man. A native of Appalachia, he splits his time between his hometown of Hyden and nearby Lexington, Kentucky. His work has been published in several anthologies and various publications. He is a regular contributor to HumorOutcasts.com and the GoodMenProject.com. He lives with his husband Andy, and their two dogs, Duke and Dudley.

Humor Inspiration: Tim Jones

My style of humor writing draws heavily from what is known as "observational humor" – looking at everyday situations most of us have experienced, sometimes with frustrating outcomes, and culling them for the humor I can find. I try to look at everyday situations most people have been through, like the frustration of teaching your teenager how to drive, or conducting a yard sale, or the hassles of airline travel, or entering Costco, intending to buy only groceries but coming out with a 56" High Def flat screen TV.

When writing about my own experiences, I often exaggerate – sometimes to preposterous extremes. But there is almost always a large kernel of truth, with which I am hoping the reader can identify and say to themselves, "Yeah, been there; done that." I often write about mundane things that happened to me and look for a way to make my experience relatable to the average reader. For example, recently, I took my teenage daughter around to a couple dozen car dealerships to help her purchase her first car. She didn't know the first thing about car buying. The actual two-day car shopping experience was exhausting, frustrating and at times infuriating. It's from these sorts of "everyman" experiences that I draw a lot of my humor.

One of my preferred approaches to humor writing is to find a topic that I know almost nothing about – say, how to solve our nation's debt crisis – and then pontificate as if I were the foremost authority on the issue, proceeding to offer up seriously misguided advice. I am not afraid to pretend to be an expert on just about any subject. Especially parenting. I have written many posts in which I offered up "expert advice" on how to be a better parent, pulling heavily from my own egregious mistakes in that arena. Case in point, a piece I wrote called "Always Lie to Your Kids." Thankfully, my kids have never really paid much attention to what I have to say, and that includes my humor writing, so they're fine about it.

In the end, I think it's not the challenges, frustrations and disappointments that we all experience day in and day out in life that matter so much as how we let them impact us. I choose, through my writing, to laugh at my life's frustrations, mistakes and failures – and laugh at myself – and hopefully, in the process, help others to do the same. That's why I write. It sure isn't for the money.

You can find the work of Tim Jones on HumorOutcasts.com as well as his popular blog ViewFromTheBleachers.net. His first book YOU'RE GROUNDED FOR LIFE-Misguided Parenting Strategies That Sounded Good At The Time has received rave reviews from parents in all stages of life, who after reading Tim's book, now feel much better about their child-rearing choices.

Humor Inspiration: Jen Tucker

Humor is everywhere. It's in the day-to-day, the mundane, your Great Dane—you get the picture. The thing about finding what's funny is choosing to see it. Laughs can be obvious, like when your kindergartner has planned her one-sided nuptials to Matt Lauer. Others may take a little distance to tickle your funny bone, such as the debacle at the post office that may have earned you a ranking on a certain list—not that I'd know anything about that scenario.

From puns to dirty jokes, what makes something funny? That, my friend, is up to the funny bone. For me, seeing the humor in life is what gets me through. I believe humor can be the silver lining in situations, making an appearance when we look for ways to cope, relieve stress, or escape the curveballs life throws our way. If you can see through the muck and mire of your own circumstances and grasp onto humor, I think you're one step ahead of the game. Humor is a universal language. Speak it!

Humorist Jen Tucker is a writer of films, commercials, columns, books, grocery lists, and lunchbox love notes. Her memoir, The Day I Wore My Panties Inside Out was a 2011 Goodreads semifinalist in the humor category. She is a proud member of HumorOutcasts, where her writings have been featured. Her musings have appeared on Survival for Blondes, Erma Bombeck Writers Workshop, Survival Mom, and Apraxia Mom. Jen lives in Indiana with her ever-patient husband, three moxie-filled children, and two flight-risk golden retrievers.

Humor Inspiration: Billy Dees

Good humor is much like good music. Are there some certain criteria for it? Probably not, but when you hear it, you know it. If you're like me, a good pop song entertains the soul as much as a great classical composition. It really is a matter of what the overall artistic message is and how it's packaged.

I am able to enjoy a "dirty joke" as much as any other carnivorous male of the human species. However, if you ask me about the gag the next day, it is very possible I will not remember it. What humor will I remember? The answer is the same for any standup routine, sitcom, or silly romantic comedy. The best humor provides observations and insights into human behavior as we react to life's curious and sometimes ironic circumstances.

This is a general principle that I try to apply to all of my writing and creative endeavors. Is there a different perspective that the reader may not have considered yet? Especially in an ideologically driven world, it doesn't matter how well researched the subject is; rehashing the same points of view is futile. On the other hand, if you can give the audience a peek behind the curtain of a given topic your chances improve immeasurably of making an impression.

Once in a while you'll be able to make them laugh at themselves.
That's when you've really won.

Billy Dees enjoys science, news, and pop culture and is always ready for a great conversation. He is an editorialist, voice-over man, and overall creative type.
www.BillyDeesSpace.com

Humor Inspiration: Concha Alborg

In many ways writing a book with humor is similar to living life with humor. If I can see how ironic a situation is, no matter how difficult or serious, then I'm fine. Humor has saved me on many an occasion on the page and in life when I could have screamed with frustration.

Take the day that I had to go to the post office to pick up a package. I love Philadelphia, but mail delivery living in Center City can be a frustrating experience. One needs to be at home at the precise moment the mailman arrives as if he were Prince Charming. If you miss him, your package ends up in the Central Post Office, where the lines are long and slow and there is no place to park within four or five city blocks.

It was Valentine's Day, the first Hallmark holiday since my cheating husband had died. I had been warned how difficult each first event as a new widow would be. The holiday package turned out to be the Don Juan's ashes! No, it wasn't flowers or candy. I wouldn't be having a romantic evening with him either. I hadn't fixed his favorite Spanish dish. There was no sweet little gift waiting for him, not even a corny card saying how much I loved him. But there I was walking arm in arm, so to speak, with my late Valentine. Such a small package for a man with such a big ego!

I took advantage of the unexpected coziness to tell him that I had found out about his affairs, that I wasn't grieving for him but for the happy marriage I thought we had. I told him that, ironically, I felt free on this my first holiday without him. My first and his last, that was certain.

Humor helped me write about life as a modern widow, dating on the Internet and surviving to tell the stories. Humor makes a terrible situation into something more palatable. Humor saved me.

To read more about this relationship, see *Divorce after Death. A Widow's Memoir.*

Concha Alborg earned an MA from Emory University and a PhD in Spanish Literature from Temple University. In addition to numerous academic publications on contemporary women writers, she has been actively writing fiction and creative non-fiction. Recently, she left Saint Joseph's University, where she was a professor for more than twenty years, to write full time. She has published two collections of short stories: Una noche en casa (Madrid, 1995) and Beyond Jet-Lag (New Jersey, 2000) and a novel, American in Translation: A Novel in Three Novellas (Indiana, 2011).

Humor Inspiration: Eric Hetvile

I am mainly attracted to things that I feel are, on the surface, completely absurd to me, but maybe not yet seen that way by many people. Sometimes you need a humorous nudge further down the road to maybe see things in a slightly different light. This usually brings me to religion and politics. These are two areas where people sort of operate on auto-pilot. I don't think you could get a lot of people to buy into a story about a guy coming back from the dead in 2016. But since it happened a long time ago, it's somehow more believable. Resurrection: yes, indecipherable golden plates in a cave: no. And many stories are well established as somehow uplifting, when in reality when given a fresh look, are horribly screwed up. "Biblemania—The Story of Job" and "Biblemania— The Story of Lot" are some pieces where I explore these tales. I also am drawn to the constant idea that God was "looking out for" people who went through horrible circumstances and barely lived. "Man Paralyzed and Left for Dead Pretty Sure God Has Special Plan for Him." Or the fact that some metal in a deadly explosion was twisted in the shape of a cross? Gee, thanks.

Some recent examples concern some "conservative" issues in the news. Some southern states rose up angrily to protest any possible refugees coming to their states. So I tried to turn that on its head in "Syrian Refugees Refusing to Move to Texas, Louisiana, or Alabama." What if the refugees would rather take their chances with ISIS than have to live in Texas?

And I constantly see people complaining about what some poor person might or might not be eating with food stamps.

Where does it end? What would make people happy? "New Missouri Law Requires Those on Public Assistance to Wear Burlap Sacks." But basically just random stuff.

Eric Hetvile is a devout atheist and liberal who never hides from controversy with his social commentary. An original member of the HumorOutcasts.com family, Eric has the honor of generating the most hate mail for HumorOutcasts.com editors. But we still love him.

Humor Inspiration: Paul De Lancey

I use humor because I love to make people laugh. Sometimes, though, the subject is so serious that you either laugh or cry. I choose to laugh. I also add humor to a subject because I have to be different than other writers. I need to add something to the genre. My cookbook, *Eat Me*, is an example of this. The humorous tidbits I add at the end of each recipe make the cookbook enjoyable as well as informative.

However, there are some instances where I've found it is unwise to use humorous writing; letters to law enforcement and the IRS come to mind. I actually find it quite easy to inject, not infest as some detractors might claim, humor into writing. I mean, how could one make bun cha, a Vietnamese entree, and not wonder if man buns caused the Cuban Revolution? Or not contemplate opportunities in the stock market after a nuclear war? Assuming you'd survive, that would be a real laugh-or-cry moment. Again, I'd choose to laugh. I would always choose to laugh, unless of course, the only food remaining in apocalyptic times was lutefisk. So there you have it. Laugh and the world will laugh with you or at you. In either case, your audience will be so enthralled with you that they'll stop dreaming up ways to create bank fees or make airline travel miserable. And for that shining moment, you will have done humanity a great service.

Paul De Lancey is known as HumorOutcasts.com's comic chef as well as the presidential candidate for the Bacon & Chocolate Party. He writes in multiple genres: adventure, westerns, morality, time travel, thriller, and culinary, all spiced with zaniness. His cookbook, Eat Me, 169 Fun Recipes from All Over the World and his novels Beneficial Murders, We're French and You're Not and The Fur West have won acclaim from award-winning novelists. His latest work (Do Lutheran Hunks Eat Mushrooms?) shows us how Armageddon might be unleashed when the Devil and a supermarket cashier conspire to trick a man into eating a mushroom. Paul is also the writer of hilarious articles and somewhat drier ones in economics. Dr. De Lancey obtained his Doctorate in Economics from the University of Wisconsin. His thesis, Official Reserve Management and Forecasts of Official Reserves, disappears from bookstore shelves so quickly that most would-be purchasers can never find it in stock.

Humor Inspiration: John Chamberlin

I guess the one thing that inspires my sense of humor is the fact that I am first to laugh at myself. For example, I can't dance. Well, maybe I think that I can after a little bit of alcohol. So, just like the 6th grade dance, as an adult, I stand along a wall or sit in a back corner at weddings and parties and make fun of the people that are dancing poorly. My excuse for doing that is I know full well that, if I were watching me dance, or if others were watching me dance, we'd all be making fun of me! "Is he hearing the same song the rest of us are hearing?" So I'm taking my shot when I can.

Secondly, I am inspired by the underdogs of life. I hate it when people are rude to others or think of themselves as "too good" for the rest of us. I'm pretty confident in myself, but I could never be so confident that I could be snooty. Okay, maybe I can be snooty about crispy French fries, but, ok, wait, maybe peanut butter, but that's about it.

Is it my God-given right to poke fun at others that act like Jagoffs? Probably not, but I figure, the first step in being legit is pointing at myself when necessary, and then, I have some "street cred" to go out and see the humor going on, i.e. poke fun at others. And when I do poke fun, I try to stretch the reality a bit and then, just a bit more. For example, should the dumb bank robber have robbed the bank with his face in plain sight? No, he should have worn a mask. No wait, too late for that, but at least I can suggest that he uses one of those crazy SnapChat filters for his mug shot!

John Chamberlin is the author of the award-winning humor book Above the Fries. Born and raised in the Pittsburgh area, loyal denizen John Chamberlin has carved out a niche writing and talking about Jagoffs, i.e. stupid politicians, awful sports officials, dumb criminals, bad drivers, ignorant people and so on. He is the creator/writer of www.YaJagoff.com and the YaJagoff Podcast.

Humor Inspiration: Con Chapman

Groucho Marx once asked a female contestant on his TV show *You Bet Your Life* if she had any children, to which the woman responded "Yes—eight." Groucho gave her his familiar double-take and then said, "Lady, I like my cigar, but I take it out of my mouth every now and then."

I may know something about writing humor books in the way that woman knew something about producing children. I've written forty-five of them, most recently *Scooter & Skipper Blow Things Up!* (HumorOutcasts Press). I can tell you how to start writing humor books, but as with my seemingly inexhaustible desire to eat yogurt-covered raisins, I can't tell you how to stop.

Many humorists follow the advice of F. Scott Fitzgerald to budding authors— "Write what you know." They mock those near and dear to them because there's no long-distance travel involved. You can be home for dinner every night—in fact you may miss out on some prime material if you spend time clinking cocktail glasses at fashionable watering holes trying to find an agent instead of returning home to your spouse/significant other/dominatrix.

That's how I got my start, making fun of Presbyterians, and Midwesterners, and Bostonians, and intellectuals, four basic food groups of my daily life. Eventually, however, the people you love rebel, and so you must venture further afield. In my case to India, which I've written a humor book about even though the closest I've ever come to that particular sub-continent was an Indian restaurant down the street from my apartment, which I accused of stealing my cat to make a curry dish that tasted like chicken. Don't ask me how I know my cat tasted like chicken.

I've also written about outer space, the UN, and the Federal Reserve, subjects that were just lying there—like loose footballs on an open field—waiting to be written about with tongue-in-cheek because other humorists were too busy with shopworn subjects such as handyman projects, politics and their beer-drinking habits.

What—you haven't heard of any of my books? Go back and read the title: I didn't say I'd teach you how to write a successful humor book.

Con Chapman's humor is available in print and Kindle format on amazon.com. He is currently writing a biography of Johnny Hodges, Duke Ellington's long-time alto sax player, for Oxford University Press.

Humor Inspiration: Thomas Sullivan

Of all the things to remember about life, the most important to remember is that it's absurd. It's designed that way. There's nothing you can do to change that, try as you may. We have to acknowledge that (which is not futility; it's acceptance).

I received a primer on this fact early in life. I was the youngest child in a family with four kids. I had three older sisters. Take a moment to let that sink in. It proves my point about absurdity. A wise god pursuing "intelligent design" would never arrange things this way. Only one gunning for absurdity would.

According to my mom, the first words out of my mouth were "I'm totally outnumbered here." Here are a few things older sisters do when they're bored:

- Braid your hair (so you look like a little, white version of Snoop Dogg).
- Tickle you until you wet your pants.
- Tie you to a tree and hose you down.

My first few years were basically spent as a Ken doll. Which is why I write humor stories. I need to keep reminding myself that things aren't meant to be reasonable. They aren't meant to work. A sane person isn't meant to be President – Donald Trump is. And, hopefully, while I try to keep myself level and unfrustrated, I can help remind other people of the absurd truth through my stories.

And don't worry; it doesn't get better. I'm almost fifty and nothing has changed from those Ken doll days. Consider this quick example of how things really function:

The other day was the first sunny, mid-70's day in Seattle. I spent much of the day weeding and mulching in the back yard. I trimmed some shrubs and planted a few plants. After a few hours of work, I was done. The yard was sparkling, like something in a *Sunset* Magazine photo shoot. I was ready to relax in the sun and the quiet. So I grabbed a beer and lowered into a lawn chair, ready to watch the sky while little birds chirped.

Two seconds after landing in the chair, it started. My neighbor (the one who almost always wears a Ken Griffey, Jr. Seattle Mariners jersey despite the fact that Griffey retired six years ago) brought his new and untrained puppy into the yard. And then bailed. The little guy started howling and just wouldn't stop.

Though dejected by the turn of events, I felt for the little guy. And it all made total sense. Who knows why things operate this way? Perhaps the reason there's so much absurdity is so we appreciate and enjoy things when they work right. Maybe that's the point. Regardless, sharing those stories beats brooding about them. Every time.

Thomas Sullivan is the author of So Much Time, So Little Change available on Amazon.com. He is a writer for HumorOutcasts.com and lives in Seattle.

Humor Inspiration: Stacey Roberts

Laughter lifts a burden.

Before babies learn to walk, speak, eat with utensils, pull the tails of unsuspecting house pets, lay waste to entire rooms in a matter of seconds, and how to properly use the F-word, they know two things: how to go to the bathroom in their pants and how to laugh. Humor must be an essential human thing because newborns can laugh.

I try to make anything I write funny whenever possible. Even if it is a dramatic subject. Outside of afternoon soap operas, no one can be serious all the time. The ability to be funny can humanize even the most dastardly villain. It can bring a small measure of joy to desperate circumstances. It can make friends, however briefly, out of lifelong enemies.

Unlike mysteries, thrillers, or romances, the humor genre is one in which the reader can read a book over and over again. Some things will always be funny. We should write about them.

Stacey Roberts is the author of Trailer Trash, With a Girl's Name. www.trailertrashbook.com

Humor Inspiration: Forrest Brakeman

I have to confess that I didn't really set out to write humor, or even incorporate comedy into my work. I thought I was creating heady, provocative material for the intelligentsia that straddled the line between intellectually snooty and *New Yorker* esoteric. Apparently I missed the mark by a long shot because people started laughing at me. So rather than take offense and endlessly lash out in op-ed pieces, or withdraw and pout in the corner, I went with it.

It was a helluva lot easier than rewriting everything.

Forrest is a former stand-up comedian, half of the ancient comedy team of Proops & Brakeman. After training with the Groundlings, he founded the improv comedy group Los Angeles Theatresports, where he performed and served as Co-Artistic Director. Forrest has performed at The Comedy Store and The Laugh Factory in Los Angeles, The Punch Line and Cobb's Pub in San Francisco, and has appeared on The Tonight Show and The Sunday Comics. His essays have been published in the Los Angeles Times, Huffington Post, Scary Mommy/The Mid, Boomer Cafe, the Los Angeles Daily News, NPR's "This I Believe," and the Chicago Cubs Yearbook (you heard me).

Humor Inspiration: Theresa Wiza

Almost everything inspires my humor, but mostly: unexpected outbursts (like the time my {then 6-year-old} grandson, who, when he discovered I was 60, said, "Wow! I'm surprised you're not dead yet!"); sudden changes in facial expressions (especially in kids after they're told something surprising or unbelievable); absurdities; inconsistencies; exaggerations (a family trait); contradictions; nonsense (I'm always trying to make sense out of it); altered perspectives (especially my own – I have a tendency to jump to conclusions and then realize my jumping-off point was solar systems away from where it was supposed to be); childish antics (especially in myself and other adults {esp. politicians}); kids (esp. my grandkids); me – my distracted mind often lands me in hilarious situations (like the time I became obsessed with a missing {might I add luxuriously soft} blanket and came to the conclusion, after unsuccessful searching, that neighbors had to have snuck into my home to steal it, leaving my other valuables behind, because it was SO soft – valuable lesson learned, though – obsessive hyper-focus defeats distraction); funny videos of animals and children; unexpected creative connections I make with other creative people; humorous stories and anecdotes (like those found on HumorOutcasts.com); comedy routines; old TV shows (*I Love Lucy, Everybody Loves Raymond, Friends,* and others); new TV shows (*Life in Pieces, Rush Hour, Mom,* and others); *America's Funniest Home Videos*; YouTube; emotional outbursts to physical mishaps (I don't want to laugh when somebody falls down, but…); and my own thoughts.

Find Theresa Wiza on HumorOutcasts.com and Writing Creatively (www.writingcreatively.org).

Humor Inspiration: E.V. Erton

I grew up in Liverpool, England, a gritty, blue-collar port city with a brand of humor as unique as the scouse (as Liverpudlians are known) accent. Humor is used to take the edge off life's harshness and to give a middle finger to adversity or authority in a city well-known for its renegade tendencies. Here are a couple of examples. During World War II Liverpool was pummeled by German bombers to such an extent that for many years after the city was deeply scarred. It was common to see rows of old houses with gaps where buildings had been felled by bombs. Scousers turned this spectacle into a description of a rugged smile with the well-known city expression: "he had teeth like a row of bombed houses." The class system is often the butt of scouse jokes. When The Beatles played a Royal Command Performance at the London Palladium attended by the Queen Mother and her entourage, John Lennon told the audience, "People in the cheaper seats clap your hands; the rest of you rattle your jewelry."

This type of irreverent humor that turns orthodoxy on its head inspires my work. And being scouse leaves me little choice but to poke fun at the world. Over the years I've come to value this heritage more and more. At a time when social and political divisions seem insurmountable, the power of a pithy observation to crack the Berlin Wall of prejudice is more important than ever. I particularly appreciate anecdotes that celebrate quick-witted skullduggery. Like the old Liverpool joke about a dockworker who was leaving the docks having finished his shift. Scouse longshoremen were infamous for purloining items of cargo—no matter how impractical. This guy was walking out of the dock gates with a bale of cotton on his shoulder. A security cop stopped him and asked why he was shouldering a bale of cotton. The dockworker immediately gave the cop a pained look and said, "I've an ear ache."

E. V. Erton's career as a writer spans blogging, books and short stories, corporate communications, journalism, plays and comedy sketches, satirical essays, and TV documentaries. Possibly the best way to trace his career path is to dip a sugared-up fly with ADHD in ink, and let the insect wander around a blank sheet of paper.

He lives in Pennsylvania with his wife, two kids, and a dog called Spike, who should be named Obnoxious.

Humor Inspiration: Robin Savage

I am inspired by comedians who use their powers of comedy for good. It is easy to make light of the vulnerable. Easy laughs come from making fun of those who are weaker than the rest of us. What is hard is standing up for what you believe in, even if it isn't popular. Comedy, when used properly, cuts through the status quo. It can be used as a flashlight, shining on society and exposing what we may not otherwise see. Many people credit George Carlin and Bill Hicks for being the types of comedians that questioned the rules of the establishment and changed the way that many people saw our government. I see the rise of Amy Schumer, Tina Fey and Amy Poehler as funny, smart women standing up for women in that same way. They are bringing a fresh perspective on feminism and Women's Rights.

I also think humor is as much of a survival instinct as our fight-or-flight response is. It is the sober voice in a sea of insanity letting us know everything will all be all right. So many times humor is used to soften a blow or to deflect what life has thrown our way. It is the most powerful weapon that humans have in their personal arsenal. I remember the evening of 9/11/01. I turned to the late night shows in hopes of finding some sort of release. I wondered how the talk show comedians were going to make such a tragic event palatable. I needed to feel that despite the horrid events, someway, somehow, we would be able to get through this awful day. Unfortunately, that didn't happen, at least not on that particular evening. The whole nation mourned, even the funny people. I remember being even more scared, thinking if I couldn't fall back on humor and get that reassurance, maybe we were in big trouble after all. I remember the first Saturday Night Live that was aired shortly after the terrorist attacks. Rudy Giuliani giving a whole nation permission to laugh again was historic and healing.

Robin Savage is a mother of two school-aged children by day and a Stand-Up comedian by night. She has been known to mix the two up and offer her kids a two-item minimum while helping a heckler with his homework. Robin has played comedy clubs and festivals across the country. She won a Best Actress award for a comedy short that she co-wrote in the 2014 St. Pete Comedy Film Festival. When Robin isn't performing comedy, she can be seen, late at night, Googling her own name. Robin's first book, Stand Up and Be a Lady, detailed her life as a standup comic.

Humor Inspiration: Suzette Martinez Standring

Humor writing can be learned, but it's easier if it comes naturally, like dimples or say, a lazy eye. Love, light and laughter are fun to share, a second nature. Yet the ease I felt made me struggle. I secretly wondered if humor was a cop-out genre. After all, others wrote about the big-ticket items: genocide, crime, racism, and politics.

In comparison, sharing that my husband nearly electrocuted himself with the new electric hedge clippers felt a bit petty. Long ago, when people asked me what I did, I'd say almost sheepishly, "I'm a humor columnist." As if I were in a clown suit at a funeral home, juggling. I imagined people were thinking, "Get serious and make a real difference in the world!"

Then I discovered a purpose and pride to humor writing.

I am a San Francisco native who landed a job (with no journalism experience) at a regional New Jersey newspaper in 1998. When assigned to cover the county board, I said, "No, I can't. I don't know anything about county politics. The county fair, maybe." My new editor pooh-poohed me. "Now scoot," he said. So I covered regional politics, elections, and the white-hot-button deer overpopulation problem. Most saw deer as all-munching, crop-damaging, disease-carrying pests to be culled and killed. New to wildlife, I'd get all shiny-eyed as if I had spotted a group of gorillas in my backyard. I was stressed.

To counteract it all, I wrote a humor column, seeing the county through a new resident's eyes, like how locals give directions based on landmarks that are not there. "Oh, you go right where the old

Smith house used to be." Or the strange business names: "Is there a convenience store near here?" "Yeah, the WaWa." "I'm sorry, the What-What?"

Humor writing was my therapy and I pursued it when I relocated to Massachusetts. Yet I still felt insecure, as if making funny fodder was not important enough work.

Then September 11 happened. The black smoke pouring out of the Twin Towers in New York suffocated my soul, and our national grief and mourning overcame me. The collective darkness was so vast I wondered if writing something comical could ever be appropriate again. I lost my ability to laugh for a long time. The sorrow was that deep.

Then I pulled an unread book from my shelf, *Me Talk Pretty One Day*, by David Sedaris. Soon the tears were streaming down my face. His hilarious observations on dysfunctional family, human nature and his own shortcomings made me guffaw against my will. In the middle of darkness, Sedaris forced me to laugh. I had no choice.

Epiphany: humor writing is a public service, a rare brand of healing, as effective as setting a broken bone. I now understand my own gift in the light of purpose: to dispense the healing power of laughter. More folks should take that mission on.

Suzette Martinez Standring is a syndicated columnist with GateHouse Media. She authored The Art of Opinion Writing: Insider Secrets from Top Op-Ed Columnists, an Amazon bestseller and a First Place winner in the 2014 New England Book Festival. She also wrote The Art of Column Writing and both books are used in national journalism courses, including courses at Johns Hopkins University. Her blog took First Place for on-line blogs in the 2013 National Society of Newspaper Columnists' competition. Suzette is a past president of The National Society of Newspaper Columnists and the host and producer of It's All Write With Suzette, a cable TV show about writing. She teaches writing workshops nationally.

Visit www.readsuzette.com.

Humor Inspiration: Kathy Minicozzi

What inspires my humor? It's hard for me to say, because the answer is just about anything. As a kid, I had to learn not to laugh at things that, according to everyone else, were not funny. My parents called me "Smartie" as often as they called me by my real name, and they were not referring to intelligence. A natural talent for sardonic remarks, along with a tendency to tell it as I saw it, got me loads of attention from Mom and Dad, although most of the time they weren't laughing.

Inspiration for funny writing comes to me, more often than not, during those times when my mind is ruminating, alighting on different things. The results are pieces about childhood memories, Christmas, aging, life in New York City and/or The Bronx, home decorating, fairy tales, a parody of *Jurassic World*, plain old silliness and a book about opera and the people who perform it. Some humorists find inspiration on the Internet. Others find it in everyday life, politics or the news. I am liable to pick it out of anything that comes my way or enters my imagination, and I don't know from one day to the next what I'll come up with. This is probably confusing to people, but I can't help it. One of these days, I'll find that elusive "voice" that writers talk about. Maybe I've already found it. Well, if I don't know where my "voice" is, it's obvious that nobody else does. It's probably hiding in the closet, along with that pair of boots that I never wear.

To be able to write funny is to be able to write about painful things in a way that makes them bearable. Serious writing can bring up some hard-core depression, which is probably why so many writers end up as alcoholics, drug addicts or suicides. Humor can heal that pain, or, at least, give it a different, and not so bad, perspective.

It's also a lot of fun to make people laugh.

Kathy Minicozzi is an opera singer in her 60s turned aspiring writer, who lives somewhere in New York City. In other words, she's weird, but harmless. She is the author of Opera for People Who Don't Like It, in which she turns the world of opera and its performers upside down while, at the same time, making it understandable to non-opera lovers and making everyone laugh.

Humor Inspiration: Maureen Sullivan

"I haven't laughed this hard in a long time. I actually hurt from laughing. I can't thank you enough."

That was the day I, a nurse, became a nurse humorist. I had just performed a comedy skit on stage, at a fundraiser for the American Cancer Society. The club owner called me over and asked me to please go check on the lady in the corner and see if she was feeling okay. He said she looked like she was in pain and he didn't know if he should call 911.

I walked over to this lady, who looked frail and tired, with her oxygen tubing in place. She looked like she was guarding her rib cage. For a minute I, too, thought she needed medical attention. (The fundraiser had many cancer patients in the audience who were currently undergoing chemotherapy/radiation. Odds were that some of them might be too exhausted to enjoy the show.) As I walked towards her—mind you, I went on stage in a full nurse's uniform and talked about the craziness of healthcare nowadays—she reached out, grabbed my hand, and thanked me. She thanked me! She said it had been quite a while since she had laughed, period, and tonight she laughed so hard her rib cage was actually hurting. Then, she thanked me again, stating, "It felt wonderful to laugh again."

That night defined my comedy career. I "donated" my time for the fundraiser, I spoke freely about the craziness of healthcare, and people laughed at me and with me. Laughter leveled the playing field. Best of all, an audience of cancer patients, all facing a healthcare crisis, with countless reasons to feel depressed, hopeless, isolated and frustrated....... found reason to laugh.

As a nurse humorist, I pride myself on the belief that "laughter heals." The medical research has shown that laughter improves the immune system, lowers blood pressure, releases healthy endorphins and more. In a time when healthcare may not be able to "cure" an ailment, I now have yet another skill set to improve the general public's health and well-being. It costs nothing- no co-pays or deductibles, no pre-authorization required. I consider my comedy performances a part of preventive healthcare.

My audiences may be entertained, but I am truly blessed.

Maureen Sullivan has been a Registered Nurse for over 30 years. Most of her clinical experience has been in Emergency and Trauma medicine. In the past few years she has become more focused on education. Her Irish wit and sense of humor make her a very entertaining and engaging speaker. She has done everything from individual teaching to speaking to an audience of several thousand. Her expertise is in diabetes education, stroke education and prevention, and all aspects of emergency medicine. She is also a BLS instructor and an experienced legal consultant. Maureen is the author of Listen Up!: Your guide to everything you ever wanted to know about your hospital stay and Never Again! From horror to humor, my life as a nurse.

Maureen Sullivan, MS, BSN, RN, CEN, CDE
www.MaureenSullivanRN.com

About the Author:

Donna Cavanagh is founder of HumorOutcasts.com (HO) and the partner publishing company, HumorOutcasts Press which now includes the labels Shorehouse Books and Corner Office Books (HOPress-Shorehousebooks.com). Cavanagh launched HO as an outlet for writers to showcase their work in a world that offered few avenues for humor. HO now features the creative talents of more than 100 aspiring and accomplished writers, producers, comics and authors from all over the world. Known for its eclectic content, HumorOutcasts has something for everyone. As a writer herself, Cavanagh is a former journalist who made an unscheduled stop into humor more than 20 years ago. Her syndicated columns helped her gain a national audience when her work landed in the pages of *First* Magazine, *USA Today* and other national media. She has taught the how-to lessons of humor, blogging and publishing at The Philadelphia Writers' Conference and the Erma Bombeck Writer's Workshop. Cavanagh has penned four humor books *Reality: Fantasy's Evil Twin, Try and Avoid the Speed Bumps, A Canine's Guide to the Good Life* (which she wrote with her dogs Frankie and Lulu) and the USA Books Contest finalist *Life On the Off Ramp*. Cavanagh hopes her latest book *How to Write and Share Humor: Techniques to Tickle Funny Bones and Win Fans* will encourage writers not only to embrace their humor talents but show them off as well. She lives in the Philly suburbs with her husband Ed and her two author dogs.

Made in the USA
Charleston, SC
02 December 2016